Praise for THE TERRIBLE THREES

"Hilarious! Race through this book in a public place only if you don't mind laughing and spitting on yourself in front of strangers. Reed is the Mike Tyson of conspiracy-theory comedy. He never pulls a punch."
—Trey Ellis, author of *Platitudes*

"Reed is without a doubt our finest satirist since Mark Twain."
—*Washington Post*

"Like all great American comic spirits from Louis Armstrong to Curly Howard of the Three Stooges, from Richard Pryor to Zora Neale Hurston, Reed relentlessly deciphers his culture, subverts it really. . . . *The Terrible Threes* seems a work that he could not avoid writing."—Gerald Early, *New York Times*

"Never a dull moment with Reed . . . even Reed's enemies place him in the canon of black male writers with Richard Wright, Ralph Ellison, and Amiri Baraka."—*San Francisco Examiner*

"A jazzlike, surreal phantasmagoria. . . . An uproarious, wisecracking, deadly serious farce . . . when Reed is on target, which is much of the time, he is one of the sharpest socio-political satirists around, hurling pointed barbs at racism, the CIA, women, the Vatican, the New York literary crowd and Americans' demand for instant gratification."—*Publishers Weekly*

"A great writer."—James Baldwin

"Reed's writing is fierce and funny . . . there's hardly a topic that escapes his scathing pen."—*Essence*

"A talent for hyperbole and downright yarning unequaled since Mark Twain. . . . Reed is a one-of-a-kind writer."—*Saturday Review*

"Ishmael Reed is probably the best black writer in America today."
—*Village Voice*

"Reed, with undiminished fervor, forces readers to both laugh and cry over the less-than-noble ways and means of late-twentieth-century America. The novel is a scream—but sobering, too."—*Booklist*

DISCARD

P9-DCN-149

BY ISHMAEL REED

ESSAYS

Writin' Is Fightin'
God Made Alaska for the Indians
Shrovetide in Old New Orleans
Airing Dirty Laundry

NOVELS

Japanese by Spring
The Terrible Threes
Reckless Eyeballing
The Terrible Twos
Flight to Canada
The Last Days of Louisiana Red
Mumbo Jumbo
Yellow Back Radio Broke-Down
The Free-Lance Pallbearers

POETRY

New and Collected Poems
A Secretary to the Spirits
Chattanooga
Conjure
Catechism of D Neoamerican Hoodoo Church

PLAYS

Mother Hubbard, *formerly* Hell Hath No Fury
The Ace Boons
Savage Wilds
Hubba City

ANTHOLOGIES

The Before Columbus Foundation Fiction Anthology
The Before Columbus Foundation Poetry Anthology
Calafia
19 Necromancers from Now
Multi-America: Essays on Cultural War and Cultural Peace

THE TERRIBLE
THREES

ISHMAEL REED

Dalkey Archive Press

Copyright © 1989 by Ishmael Reed
First Dalkey Archive edition, 1999
All rights reserved

Library of Congress Cataloging-in-Publication Data:

Reed, Ishmael, 1938-
    The terrible threes / Ishmael Reed. — 1st Dalkey Archive ed.
    p. cm.
    ISBN 1-56478-224-7 (alk. paper)
    1. United States—Politics and government—Fiction. I. Title.
    PS3568.E365T37 1999
    813'.54—dc21
                                99-35666
                                 CIP

This publication is partially supported by grants from the Lannan Foundation, the
Illinois Arts Council, a state agency, and the National Endowment for the Arts, a
federal agency.

Dalkey Archive Press
Illinois State University
Campus Box 4241
Normal, IL 61790-4241

visit our website at: www.dalkeyarchive.com

Printed on permanent/durable acid-free paper and bound in the United States of America.

To Steve Cannon,
whose novel will change
American fiction.

When turkeys mate, they think of swans.

—*Johnny Carson*

Black Peter Calypso

His family had no food stamps
and didn't have no tree
The projects were their humble home
in New York on Avenue D
Don't worry mom we'll supper
can't promise you no lamb
Black Peter went to reform school
for stealing a Xmas ham
for stealing a Xmas ham

He worked a smart street hustle
around Eighth avenue
He plied a little dummy
he threw his voice into
A vagrant stole his dummy
the thing he used to earn
He joined the Nic-o-la-ites
He had no place to turn
He thought for a brief sojourn
He thought for a brief sojourn

They fought the Xmas bosses
who turned Noel to sales
Who took Nick from the people
and gave him to the swells
They made a Nicholas dummy
he threw his voice into
It looked like old Kris Kringle
same weight same height same hue
It fought the Xmas bosses
it was their nudging foe
don't buy their ugly war toys
don't buy their flammable dolls
don't buy the mink wrapped Barbies
they push on girls and boys

This made the bosses angry
what Peter had it say
For them the month of December
was time for a big pay day
And so at Peter's party
on Seventh avenue
The bosses sent their hit men
to create a terrible din
to drive Pete to the bin
to drive Pete to the bin

and that is where he's been

Where are you now Black Peter?
the chimney's missing you
The mood of Xmas is not the same
the joy has gone from caroling
Jack Marse has taken back the fun
and killed the Xmas cheer
and killed the Xmas cheer

Preface

The Terrible Threes begins on Thanksgiving in the late nine-
teen-nineties. It's been four years since the Christmas of the
Terrible Twos, a Christmas which saw amazing events tran-
spire in the White House of Dean Clift, former fashion model,
who rose from Congressman to Vice President, and then to
the Presidency after the death of General Walter Scott, hero
of Dominica. Dean Clift was a hands-off President who didn't
know and didn't care to know about the activities of his
advisors, Admiral Matthews, Bob Krantz, Vice President Jesse
Hatch, and Reverend Clement Jones, the administration's
spiritual advisor.

Clift changed, however, after his wife, Elizabeth, the first
lady, was electrocuted while lighting the White House Christmas tree, and he was visited by Saint Nicholas, who revealed
to him the fate of former leaders, who had made terrible and
tragic mistakes. Saint Nicholas, out to remove his Protestant
image as that of a buffoon in a red suit, also warned Clift of
a covert operation, developed by Krantz, Jones, and Matthews, code-named Two Birds, a plan to rid America of
surplus people and wipe out an African country in possession

of nuclear weapons at the same time. Nobody believed Dean Clift, when he discussed his vision before a nationwide television audience, and the Twenty-fifth Amendment regarding Presidential disability was invoked to remove him from office to a private sanatorium about fifty miles from Washington. Saint Nicholas, who had hoped to change the course of history, went back to the drawing board.

Black Peter learns of an imposter Black Peter who gave the toy manufacturers a worrisome time during the Terrible Twos Christmas while a member of a sect which holds Nicholas to be divine. He emerges from Guinea, an island beneath the Caribbean Ocean, to challenge this Peter, a Risto Rasta who has been living in underground Manhattan since a riot that happened during a Christmas party at Madison Square Garden, which was precipitated by Jack Frost, and his goons, an employee of the toy manufacturers and Christmas card merchants. Nance Saturday, a wannabe detective, whom the clues are always ahead of, failed in his attempt to locate Snow Man, a hit man hired by a gangster named Joe Baby to assassinate Boy Bishop, leader of the Nicolaites.

Nance now drives a gypsy limousine, ferrying customers back and forth from La Guardia Airport to Manhattan. His ex-wife, Virginia, still has her television show.

I.R.

1

Nance Saturday agreed with Genesis, where it said that man should not be alone. He spent a lot of time interacting with his electronic playmates. He was watching his ex-wife's show. She was interviewing a woman whose hairstyle resembled that of a baby chick's. "Thanksgiving is just an excuse for all of the misogynists and femiphobes of the country to keep women over a hot stove, and in the shopping aisles, searching for bargains on turkey. The American men are fully capable of obtaining their own cranberry sauce. Most of them don't know how to carve a turkey, and so the women must also perform this chore. And so when people wish me a happy Thanksgiving, under the circumstances I wonder what there is to be so thankful about." Becky was wearing a white shirt, buttoned at the collar, tight shiny black pants, no socks, and black shoes. She folded her arms and crossed her legs. She then lit a cigarette. "I agree with you, Becky," Virginia said. "My ex-husband didn't even earn enough money to buy the turkey. He was always doing odd jobs. I paid his way through a year of law school, but then he dropped out. Now I've found a man who really knows how to carve the turkey. He's sensitive. He's considerate. And he's ten years younger than I am." To think that he spent those years sleeping next to a woman who would later tell their secrets to a nationwide audience. Her ratings were as high as those of her only rival, Okra Hippo, who had to be moved into the studio for appearances on her network by piano movers. He switched channels to watch her. An Asian-American man was speaking heatedly to an Asian-American woman. The man was furious. The camera kept cutting away to the audience of mostly white women, who were giving the man a cool response. The woman calmly sat in her chair, ignoring her debating opponent's fury. She was wearing a black suit and a man's tie. Okra asked her a question. He turned up the audio. "I think that Mr. Hamamoto's arguments are absurd. To suggest that the American government owes the Japanese-American community reparations. As usual, Mr. Hamamoto ignores the facts. He speaks of internment." An identification came on the screen. "Beechiko Mizuni." "He fails to distinguish between internment and relocation. Only a few thousand Japanese Americans were actually interned. But speaking to the larger question, I say that the United States did Japanese-American women a great favor. They removed them from homes in which they were brutalized by Japanese-American men. A far greater imprisonment, next to which relocation or internment were minor inconveniences. So instead of receiving $20,000 in compensation, Japanese Americans should be donating that amount to our generous government." The audience erupted into wild applause. The camera cut to the man. He was shaking his head sadly.

Nance didn't care about the battle between the sexes which had spilled over from the 80s into the 90s. He was A.W.O.L. from that war. He was keeping his to himself and not sticking it nowhere. The mysterious black Russian he'd been seeing before and since he and Virginia separated had also left. He remembered the last night of their lovemaking. She yelled out something that sounded like: YIBATTSA YIBATTSA.

He was on her like a coyote on a chicken that night. Limbs were flying, and the heels of feet were facing the ceiling. Their buttocks were rolling, gyrating, and at one point, when their rhythm was perfectly synchronized, he gave a nasty shift, like a potbellied flamenco dancer he'd once seen do, and she shrieked like someone who'd walked into the kitchen in Florida on Sunday morning and found an alligator on the floor. There were lots of French kisses and Russian fingers. The cognac had spilled on the floor. They were so weak that they almost missed the Soviet airliner that was to return her to her family in Kiev. She was wearing a black dress decorated with red roses, black 40s hat, and she carried a black handbag. Their sporadic love had become victim of yet another liberalizing trend in Russian politics. She was quarreling with her relatives because she wanted to claim her Tartar heritage, while they wanted to be thought of as European. A friend of the family, who'd had dinner with them, drank all of the Stoli they'd ordered, ate the red cabbage and the sturgeon, had returned to Kiev to tell her family that she had a black lover. They were very provincial people, commented upon books they hadn't read, and performances they hadn't seen. He thought he remembered her telling him that they were mathematicians. They had a dacha, housekeeper and a chauffeur, and didn't want to blow it.

Nance never seemed to get along with the parents of the women he dated. Virginia's mother took the cake. Virginia said it wasn't until she was thirty-five that her mother stopped beating her with the cord of an iron. When her relatives visited them, when they were married, he always wondered why they kept on their trench coats. One night he awoke and found that she wasn't sleeping beside him. He drove to the motel where her family was staying, and peeked into the window of the suite they'd rented. Some of his personal items lay on the table, and her sister, the one with a case of inhibited metabolism, was holding up one of his shirts and plucking a long strand of the Russian lady's coarse black hair from it, marked exhibit A. Virginia was crying. They seemed to be building up a case against him. That wasn't the only cause, but he remembered in the series of arguments they'd had before they broke up, he said that she was still shackled by her family. Afterward, he'd dated a series of European-American women, ranging from the California beauties you see modeling bikinis in *Sports Illustrated*, Herb Gold's favorites, to the black-haired, arty types who listened to Laurie Anderson and were into the Brooklyn Academy of Music. Virginia and her friends were right about European-American women. They spent a lot of time tossing their hair.

While vacationing in the Caribbean, he'd visited a museum where he came upon the painting of an ancient Carib woman. She was rotissering a pig. The lust in her eyes, as she stared at that pig, was immaculate. He fell in love with her fat lips and shining hair. She had small breasts and her legs looked as though she spent a lot of time running in and out of craters. Another painting showed her spearing a wild boar.

A few weeks later, he ran into a woman who looked just like her, at a gallery opening on the Lower East Side. She said that she was a Flipachino, from a small island in the Pacific called the Flipachines. They began to date, and for a while they were as happy as two sailors, dancing in a movie

with Anne Miller. Her mother found out about it. She began
to send strange envelopes to him. Some were filled with parts
of birds. In a large envelope covered with stamps with the
pictures of men wearing the kind of hairstyles that influenced
the punkers, he found the ear of a large rat. He told his lover
about it, and she said that her mother had always sent horrible
material to her lovers, and that her last boyfriend, Richard,
had disappeared.

One night she called to tell him that her mother had flown
in from the Flipachino Islands and wanted to have dinner
with them. That was fine with him, because after dinner
maybe they'd go to her apartment, put on some Marvin Gaye
records. Marvin Gaye would have loved her because she was
a real healer. What Martin Luther King Jr. would have called
a "Doctor." The kind that would have sent J.F.K. with his
bad back to a chiropractor. She did all the work, all you had
to do was lie there. She may not have been the kind of woman
that you found behind every great man, but she certainly was
next to him in a variety of other ways. At dinner her mother
said that she didn't see anything on the menu that appealed
to her and requested that the waiter bring her the names of
the diners. He didn't get the import of this incident until
later, when his date went to the ladies' room, and he was
left alone with her mother. Her mother didn't say anything,
but glared at him a long time. This made him uncomfortable
and he shifted in his seat. What was taking her daughter so
long in the bathroom? Finally, her mother pulled out a huge
basket made of straw, with a ship design on it, and removed
something. It was a miniature head, about the size of a
chestnut. An old wrinkled chestnut, or a prune. It was the
head of a man. The lips looked as though they had been
sewn. Richard, he said, weakly. The old woman nodded. He

went out to the parking lot and emptied his dinner on the ground. He never ate shrimp again.

That's when he entered a celibacy period. Orifices of the 90s were like those of the 80s, anyway. They were covered with Do Not Enter signs. No wonder Cupid was armed. He and others like him had had it with American women. He was hearing this from a lot of men. That American women were always kvetching and talking about being unhappy, without knowing what they were talking about. Even when they were happy they were unhappy. His Jewish dentist had become so upset with American women that he'd changed his religion to Islam, changed his name, and married an Arab woman. The newspapers were full of ads for foreign women, usually Asians. As far as Nance was concerned, somebody from outer space could have all of the American women. Virginia was safe, though. Though she had a habit of broadcasting their former intimate secrets on the air, he could count on there being nothing sexual between them. In fact, today, Thanksgiving, he was going to join her and her "beau," Phillip Wheatley, editor of the business page of the *New York Exegesis.*

2

President Jesse Hatch had been trying to arrange a meeting with Reverend Jones for three weeks, ever since Pedigree auctioneers had revealed the existence of a letter written by the late Admiral Matthews; rumor had it that if the letter were revealed a special prosecutor would have to be called in to unravel the mess and call for indictments. Inside the Oval Office, which Hatch rarely saw, Hatch paced up and down, his tie loosened, mashing cigarette butts into ashtrays, and behaving in a generally Type A manner, like Bogart in *The Maltese Falcon*. Jones expressed his annoyance with Hatch by staring disdainfully at the ashtray. Hatch got the message. He put out his cigarette. Reverend Jones listened patiently. "Goddamnit, that special prosecutor is trying to put our asses in jail, and all you have to say is pray."

"Don't worry, Jesse, it'll blow over. We have someone to take the fall. If Congress acts up we'll throw them a piece of meat. Kosher meat."

"I don't follow you," Hatch said, already calmer.

"Look at it this way, Jesse. Krantz has no family, he doesn't get along with the press, and he's Jewish. Who else would have that kind of name? So even though he converted—I baptized him personally—he's still a Jew at heart. We can say that he did it for Israel or something. You know, convince the Arabs that we're evenhanded, satisfy the Christian majority at the same time. We'll get public opinion on our side. Blame it on communism. That always works. Say that Krantz was part of some kind of worldwide communist conspiracy aligned with Satanists and Antichrists. Besides, I'm beginning to have my doubts about Krantz. He was always hanging around with the Admiral. Touring nuclear subs with him. And another thing. It's been almost four years since I brought him to Washington. He hasn't aged one bit."

"I've noticed that too. Nobody likes Krantz, anyway. He has almost as many enemies as you, I mean . . . I."

"Don't give it a second thought, Hatch. I know that I have enemies in the capital, but this town was worse than Sodom and Gomorrah before I came to town. Licentious parties attended by the press and politicians, womanizing and manizing, every possible sin that you can think of was being committed in broad daylight. Now the Marines are rounding up people and sending them to Sunday School. The Conversion Bill—when my court declares it constitutional—will drive the infidels out of the country. They will have to convert to Christianity or leave. I made the Congressmen give up their hideaways where they used to go and meet their dates, so they're mad. The Washington hostesses are mad because neither I, nor my cabinet, attend their parties. The Redskins hate me because I forbid government employees from attending football, a sport which I'm convinced has pagan roots. Lucy Artemis is mad at me because I put all of the soothsayers out of town, cutting in on her multimillion-dollar

business. The Shriners are mad because I caught them squir-
reling away funds from the crippled children's fund; the Ms.
America contest is mad because I insisted that the contestants
abandon cosmetic surgery, and Coca Cola is mad because I
revealed that Classic Coke wasn't on the up and up. Goddamnit, if anybody bumped me off everybody in town would
have a motive, but they can't get me, as hard as they try,
they can't get me. I don't smoke, don't drink, and unlike the
competition, I know how to keep my britches up. Do you
think that I'm going to let them get me like they did Nixon
and Reagan? He betrayed us worst of all. Cozying up to the
Russians in 1987 and 1988 just because his wife wanted him
to get the Nobel Peace Prize. You saw what happened to
them after they left Washington, didn't you? Snubbed by
California country-club Republicans. Ridiculed by their former supporters: car dealers and owners of beer franchises.
Why there were times when they couldn't even go to their
favorite Mexican restaurant without dining parties stalking
out, refusing to even be seen in public with them. When
one follows the ways of the Lord, Hatch, one becomes surrounded by agents of the Antichrist." Hatch thought for a
moment. He began letting it all sink in. Jones had a way of
lubricating words so that they eased through your mind without the slightest snag. So that they were easy to take. Hatch
fidgeted with the lapels of his pin-striped suit, as the preacher
smiled at him. Both were wearing Barbie pinstripes. Some
of the insiders were saying that the preacher was in a bad
way, talking to people who weren't in the room. An S.S.
officer from whom he sought advice. Some were even saying
that a mysterious Hollywood blowup was carrying out covert
operations for him. But there was no sign of that this morning.
The preacher had thought ahead.

"It's a shame that such a blunder was made on the basis of faulty intelligence."

"What do you mean, Reverend?"

"The Nigerians didn't have the bomb. The men over at the C.I.A. thought that this Yoruban Operation they kept referring to in their overseas communications had something to do with a weapon. It didn't. We're still trying to figure out what it meant. The only problem is that when the surps find out that there was a plan to devastate Miami and New York, we'll have a lot of explaining to do." Jones leaned back in his chair. He looked at his watch and yawned. So the Admiral had the last laugh. His maid discovering the letter in a wastebasket. Good thing that Krantz destroyed the backup archives, he thought.

"I'd better get going, Reverend. I feel better now that I've talked to you." Reverend Jones rose and shook the President's hand. As Hatch left Reverend Jones, he turned and said, "I'm glad to be on your team, Reverend Jones." Reverend Jones frowned. "The Lord's team, Hatch. The Lord's team."

3

It was fifteen degrees below, and the windchill factor made it feel like thirty below (the American standard of living was a few points lower than that), and everywhere you looked in the nation's cities, mobs were roaming, searching for food underneath garbage can lids and in charity soup lines, and in the homeless shelters, which had become an American way of life. In Washington, autos were stranded in shells of snow. Banks, airports, and schools were closed. So were the federal offices, but this didn't deter the mourners, wrapped in overcoats, from attending the funeral of Rear Admiral Matthews, retired, a member of the four who ruled the Jesse Hatch White House. Their power had increased after former President Dean Clift, the ex-model, had been removed from office after the scandal known as the Terrible Twos.

Admiral Matthews was part of the invisible government that carried on the affairs of state after the Clift debacle, aided by Reverend Clement Jones, a faith healer and televangelist, Robert Krantz, the White House communications officer and ex-television producer, and a man known as the King of

Beer, who during the Terrible Twos was involved in a dispute with Indians in Colorado over the rights to water, which the Indians claimed flowed from a sacred spring. The King of Beer had suddenly dropped out of sight, and the F.B.I. was still searching for him. Though Admiral Matthews provided the administration with a firm hand at the top, it was Krantz who carried out the orders. He was the one who spun and glided, stonewalled, and micromanaged. It was through his bland conniving that the Terrible Twos scandal had been, ultimately, shoved to the interior pages of the newspapers, and as the election approached pundits were saying that President Hatch would probably win by a landslide, his only possible rival being Dean Clift, who still commanded a small but dedicated following.

Reverend Jones, "spiritual leader" of the government, hated Admiral Matthews because the Admiral smoked cigarettes, didn't go to church, and was married to a former chorus girl. Though he had brought Krantz into government, he envied the close relationship that Krantz had developed with Admiral Matthews. Admiral Matthews and Krantz had been like father and son, and to think it was he, Jones, who had rescued Krantz from certain death underneath the wheels of a fiery sports car, the incident that had brought millions more to Reverend Jones's gospel hour. Reverend Jones could do what no other white preacher in America could do, and though his church had brought in millions, Jones shunned the lavish style of living embraced by his colleagues, and sometimes went about in the same polyester suit and drove a 1958 Studebaker through the streets of Washington. He seldom went home where his wife's every need was being handled by a household staff and where she passed her days doing

watercolors of the same landscape. The same tree. The same
cloud. And the same flower garden. She had done hundreds
of paintings of the same scene. The paintings filled the three
bedrooms of the upstairs, the garages and the basements.
Sometimes she would paint for three days, and go without
food. It kept her busy, and the Reverend figured that it was
good therapy.

At the Admiral's funeral Jones sat next to the widow, but
ignored her. His own wife sat on his other side, a shivering
pile of fragile bones. Eagles and flags were omnipresent,
including those belonging to the Marines. They began
the services, slowly marching down the aisles, in front of
the Admiral's coffin. After the coffin was placed in front
of the church, the pastor read the invocation. Because of
the cold in the church, there was more than the usual
amount of coughing. It sounded hollow in the huge church.
Some hymns were sung. And then the pastor introduced
Reverend Jones, who headed toward the lectern, as sturdy
as a Volkswagen bug. The media personnel outnumbered
the mourners, and Reverend Jones began to dab his face with
a handkerchief, so hot were the lights, even in the cold
church.

He began to slowly recount the story of Abraham, and
how when the old Patriarch was through and had done his
work, he was ready for his trip to the Promised Land. The
Reverend recounted how the members of the old man's tribe,
the women, and the men, and the little children, had all
stood before Abraham, and how God had promised that he
would select a leader to replace Abraham. The preacher,
with that familiar whiny voice that had excited millions of
the helpless, likened Abraham to Admiral Matthews, and

though he did not name himself as Matthews's successor, he asked the church for their prayers, as he guided America through the great tsunami that lay ahead. After Jones had warmed up he began pacing up and down the pulpit, and sliding across the pulpit like James Brown. He began to do the Al Green hop. He began to do the old black preacher's "uh huh . . . uh huh . . . huh." His voice began to become gravelly, and he began to shout for emphasis, like Jesse Jackson. He knew how to screech and say OOOOOOOOO in falsetto like Little Richard, and then his voice took on that tremulous timbre like one of the greatest black preachers of all time, Reverend E. Franklin. Even some of these women who were the mainstays of Washington society, who hated Reverend Jones, women who spent a lot of time under the dryer and preparing for lunch, women who would spend entire days shopping for clothes, convulsed, their stomachs rippling. A couple of them even "went out," and had to be assisted to the waiting ambulances that were always on hand when Reverend Jones was going to preach.

An American legend: Colonel Tom Parker was supposed to have said that if he could find a white man who could sing rock and roll like a black man, he'd make a million dollars. Elvis Presley was invented. It could also be said that if a white preacher could be found who could preach like one of the great carriers of the oral tradition, could preach like a black preacher, he would rule America. People were saying that Reverend Jones was that preacher. None of this pitiful, whining Jimmy Swaggart stuff. None of this wimpy Fulton Sheen crystal cathedral tepidness. None of this Jim Bakker Charlie McCarthy machinations, the theme parks, the positively nouveau display of wealth.

* * *

When he was on, Reverend Jones preached his gospel hour in a Texas church that held no more than 250 people, but the way he had the old sisters banging on them bass drums and slapping them tambourines, you'd think that God's Own Philharmonic was carrying on inside that old church where the loudspeakers blasted Jones's message to the thousands who stood outside. At the conclusion of Reverend Jones's sermon, the church didn't need no fire, because it was being warmed by the spirit of the Lord. By the spirit of Jesus. "Because when you got Jesus you don't need no expensive indoor heating, no oven, no nuclear fuel, no solar energy, when you got Jesus you got all the heat you need. Jesus hits like an Atomic Bomb," Jones shouted to the mourners. People began removing their overcoats. This had been the closest thing to a sermon that he'd preached since he joined the administration of Dean Clift. He didn't want to be accused of mixing religion with politics, a charge that had been made when he became part of the inner circle which Clift fronted, and so he'd turned over his multibillion-dollar ministry to a young preacher named Rev. John the Conquerer, after the vision he had in a Riverside, California, motel, when Jesus appeared to him in the form of a desk clerk and asked him to go to Washington and save America from the primeval slime, Satan worship and Prince. Hip hop, funk, astrology, etc.

4

The lettuce was flecked with stains the color of soy sauce, and the tomatoes were turning black. The roast beef was thinly sliced, dry, and white. Krantz had been to a lot of these dinners. The same old chocolate pudding. Some of the current heroes, who'd blipped across the nation's TV screens, were seated on the dais. Carson Richards, Wall Street speculator and junk bond addict, former pimp, whom the New Christians pointed to as an example of how a surp could still rise in an American society ruled by the Jesse Hatch administration, and the New Christian majority in Congress. Seated next to him was Ted Bare, the skinhead who became famous after setting a surp afire while the surp was wrapped in dirty blankets and sleeping underneath a Santa Cruz freeway. He didn't remove his Boston Red Sox baseball cap; he wore sneakers and a red, white, and blue basketball jacket. Krantz wore the uniform of the New Christian, Barbie black and white pinstripes, after the suit worn by Klaus Barbie at his trial at Lyons. Reverend Jones saw Hitler as a misunderstood genius, a sort of knight of Christianity saving the West, defending the free world from the Mongolian hordes and Asiatic death. He required that members of his team wear the Barbie outfit. They never asked why, being loyal to Reverend Jones. He never discussed his Hitlerian ideas with the staff and only shared them with his intimates, Heinrich, and Joe Beowulf, a robot superhero on loan to him from Towers Bradhurst, Hollywood producer.

Krantz successfully concealed his red eyes with drops of Murine; he'd hastily shaven in the limousine that drove him to the hotel, and had done a pretty convincing job of it, only a few hairs having been missed; you couldn't tell that he'd slept in his suit or that his shirt was drenched, or that his hands were trembling. William Manchester reported that the night before his Dallas murder (the Terrible One) President Kennedy's hands were trembling as he made a speech before a group of scornful cattlemen. The same crew that had killed him were still in the secret government; Krantz knew, for he had met with them in out-of-the-way hotels and airport rest rooms as he gave them assignments coming from the Colorado Gang, as the inner circle was being called. Would they kill him? Had they killed Admiral Matthews? Matthews was right, but he wasn't nuts. He'd always vetoed the kooky proposals that the King of Beer and the Reverend Jones had made. His sudden death was a shock because there had been no sign of illness. He and Krantz had attended a Press Club dinner the night before, and the Admiral had even been roasted.

They couldn't kill Krantz, of course, but would attempt to do so if he exposed the mission. He paused from his thoughts long enough to hear his name called. The introduction, referring to his distinguished career as a television producer of the soap opera "Sorrows and Trials," and the often-told story about how Reverend Jones had rescued him from a car accident and had miraculously delivered him from underneath its wheels—a story that had been embellished each time it had been repeated—was followed by a standing ovation as Krantz approached the microphones to deliver his speech. He made a joke about the Washington weather. Both airports were closed, and the hotel lights, though on for now, were threatening to go out. He made a joke about the Post Office, everybody's favorite bureaucratic whipping boy. About how he'd been in one of the long Xmas lines and the woman ahead of him complained about having to pay the postage for a gift she received and the price of the postage exceeding the value of the gift. He then got down to the speech. It was the speech that he'd delivered hundreds of times, about the terrible period that happened before the administration of Jesse Hatch and Reverend Jones. About how surps in running shoes and hoods had just about taken over the cities. About how the United States was being laughed at by the world for the sellout deal that left-winger Ronald Reagan had made with the Russians, the one they were calling the Second Yalta. Some on the right, himself included, had even said that Reagan, feeble and sick and under the guidance of a San Francisco astrologer, had made a verbal agreement with Gorbachev at Reykjavík, one that amounted to surrender. He talked about how administrations after that had faltered, until the election of General Walter Scott, hero of Dominica, whom he described as "a shaft of light at the bottom of the cellar." And how just as the Terribles that had begun with the assassination of J.F.K. were thought to have come to an end, General Scott died from a cold he'd contracted on In-auguration Day. And how Dean Clift had been sworn in to carry out the policies of General Scott, only to suffer "an episode of nervous exhaustion, saying that he was visited by

Saint Nicholas." The audience laughed, as usual, at this line. Krantz signaled them to cease. "It's no joke, ladies and gentlemen," he said. "It wasn't funny when he accused me, Admiral Matthews, Reverend Jones, and the King of Beer of being engaged in some sort of secret operation, therefore smearing three of the greatest patriots this country has ever known." The audience rose and gave him a standing ovation, which was the usual response to this line, until Krantz requested that they resume their seats. He dramatically mopped his brow, the hotel's generator being too hot. "Said that the four of us were in on some kind of fantasy that only existed in his mind, an Operation Two Birds, some kind of back-channel operation that, according to him, involved some rip-off artists, free-lance arms dealers, assorted and shady consultants and con men. No wonder folks began calling him President Weird.

"Oh, you know the rest, ladies and gentlemen, how the nations had to endure another Terrible. Another President crippled in office. And you know how fond we were of Dean and his lovely wife, Elizabeth. But, now that I look back at it, maybe the Lord was sending us a sign when Elizabeth was struck down by that Xmas tree. That dreadful night led to Clift's downfall, and I'm convinced that his strange recital on television about alleged wrongdoings by the Admiral, Reverend Jones, the King of Beer, and me was a result of the young man's distraught condition. That's what I thought then, but recently, ladies and gentlemen, we've learned that some of the wild rumors that had been going around about his administration were true. The P.C.P. and angel dust parties in the White House, where unrobed young men and women were entertained by the heavy metal music of Boy Gonorrhea and Frequent Urination. They were playing the music of Hell. This couple had turned the mansion into a fornicating den of Satan, ladies and gentlemen. And when we went to serve the notice to Dean Clift that he was to be removed from office, he was engaged in some bizarre Xmas tree planting that Reverend Jones, not only the greatest chief of staff in history, but a great biblical scholar as well, authority on Milton, and a member of the English Department of Queens College for ten years—before he relocated to Texas—identified as the pagan rites of Saturnalia. It wasn't the grief, ladies and gentlemen, it was some kind of wild hallucinogenic that caused him to make that speech. After we got rid of him, Jesse Hatch, a true patriot, took over and, with his aides, was able to get the country moving again.

"We tried to turn back the waves of infidels coming in over the border arriving in freedom boats into Florida; we tried to ban Spanish, and now everybody it seems is speaking it; we thought that the Asian Americans would set an example for the others, but they turned out to be as deceitful and as cunning as their ancestors described in the writings of the California prophet Jack London, who warned of the invasion of yellows. They were making millions of dollars from drug sales, and with the profits buying up the United States. And so who needs them, ladies and gentlemen? Who needs the yellows, the browns, the reds, and the blacks, unless they, like Carson Richards, serve our Western ways, preserve our values? Unless they do that, they are surps. The wastes of history, the floating dump of the eons." The audience was still as Krantz began to wind up his speech. "And now, ladies and gentlemen, Clift's trying to regain the power that the Lord wanted taken from him. He is challenging the decision that removed him from office, even though everything was legal.

"We got the majority of principal officers of the executive departments and Vice President Hatch to send a letter to Congress stating that President Clift was incapable of discharging the duties of his office. And as you know, the appeals court upheld the lower court's decision last week. And I promise you that the Supreme Court with Chief Justice Nola Payne in charge will do likewise, ladies and gentlemen, and then let us hope that Dean Clift will come to his senses and unite behind Jesse Hatch and the greatest White House chief of staff in history, Reverend Clement Jones." The audience rose and began to clap until their hands became sore. Krantz was mobbed and had to have an aisle cleared so that he could make his way from the podium to the waiting limousine in the rear of the hotel, shaking hands with dignitaries along the way. Reporters were after him with questions. *Mr. Krantz, is it true that Reverend Jones spends hours in the Oval Office talking to pretend friends? Over here, Mr. Krantz. Bob, aren't you concerned about the circumstances surrounding Admiral Matthews's death; don't you have suspicions? Mr. Krantz, is it true that you're leaving the White House for an ambassadorial post?* Krantz didn't answer any questions. He instructed the driver to get him to the White House.

5

Nance decided to make one more run from La Guardia before going to Virginia's for dinner. This time he didn't have to hustle. A man opened the door of the black limousine that Joe Baby had given him and got in. "I hope you're not in a hurry," Nance said. "I have to get at least four more passengers. It's not worth my while just to take one passenger downtown." Nance could only realize a profit when he squeezed five passengers into the car. Three on small seats that could be lifted from the floor. "I can't make any money that way." The man slipped some bills into his hand. Nance looked. Two hundred dollars. He looked over his shoulder. It was Joe Baby's partner, Big Meat.

"Big Meat," Nance said.

"I don't call myself that anymore. I'm using my real name, Carson Richards. I've put that other life behind me," he said in a tremulous baritone voice. He was wearing a fur coat, and the type of hat that bluesman Albert King wears. Dark with a shining dark band. He hadn't gotten rid of his rings. He seemed more polished. He told Nance that he wanted to be let out at the Pierre Hotel. In the last conversation he had with Big Meat, about four years before, he had told Nance that he wanted to go into a white-collar business, running a security business for tycoons like Elder Marse. Jack Frost worked for him. Nance asked him what he did for a living.

"I'm working on Wall Street."

"That's a change."

"Yeah."

"Where you coming from?" They were driving through Queens near the curious ruins that Robert Moses had left behind.

"A dinner. This neoconservative foundation just honored me. They say that I show what a surp can do if they really put their minds to it. They're making me an example. I was sitting at the head table with the people who run the country. This man who is next to President Hatch spoke. Bob Krantz. Man he had the people on their feet they were applauding so."

"How can you join that bunch? Hell, the only reason that conservatism was invented was so that some Irish guys could get into the Morocco Club. They didn't even have a phi- losophy until the 1950s."

"You're still angry, huh, Nance. Bitter. Political. That's why you're political. You never used to be political. It's because you're down on your luck. That's why you're driving this beat-up wagon. You never could settle into anything that made some money. What would you be doing if Joe Baby hadn't left you this pimp car?" Big Meat and Joe Baby were pimps together. They had an apartment and were running a call girl service that catered to the convention crowd. They were doing alright until Boy Bishop, leader of a sect that revered Saint Nicholas, recruited the whores. "You ought to get into the speculation business. If you get caught all you have to do is to pay a fine. My heroes used to be people like Nicky Barnes. Now I have a picture of Ivan Boesky on the wall. Somebody who uses his head. You remember that white boy we hired Snow Man to hit?"

"Do I remember."

"He taught me a lesson. I mean, I figured that if he could do that to me and Joe Baby, it was time for me to quit and to find something better to do than hustling some whores. Shit, I read that seven out of ten women aren't satisfied anyway. Have never achieved an orgasm. The odds are better in the junk bond business, and if you have somebody giving you tips, you win all the time. You have a head on your shoulders, Nance, yet you're into some nickel-and-dime gypsy cab operation. You let those guys take your confidence. You let them get you down. You're not living up to your full potential. You are all beaten down because you weren't able to find Snow Man. I think the guy probably took the fifty K that Joe Baby and I gave him and left town. You shouldn't blame yourself. By the way, how is Virginia doing?"

"We finally got a divorce. She's dating a young economist." Big Meat thought that this was hilarious. They turned the corner at Fifth Avenue. Xmas crowds were out, and the trees in Central Park were lit. Big Meat wished Nance a Merry Xmas and Happy New Year. He strutted into the Pierre Hotel where he was going to get a manicure. The doorman smiled at him.

6

Kingsley Scabb of the Newport Scabbs sat across from his wife. He was wearing a black blazer, white slacks with sharp creases, blue shirt, open at the collar, brown moccasins and dark blue sunglasses. One of his moles had told him of the meeting Reverend Jones had with President Hatch, and the concern they were all having about the consequences if Operation Two Birds were publicly aired. Scabb was the only one who would gain from such a scandal. Nobody could tie it to him, since he wasn't inside the loop. The inner circle. Why he was just about as much in the dark about the plan Operation Two Birds, which had become known as the Terrible Twos in the popular imagination, as Dean Clift was. The next election would be his chance. He knew from some of his White House spies that Hatch might be indicted because of an ancient land deal. Jones would like to run, but Jones knew that they would dig up some of those ancient sermons which sounded strange. His obsession about the satanic code in the dollar bill or something. Power had shifted to the Sunbelt where everything was new and crude. Dean Clift was from New York, and he had failed. So now it was time for Scabb. Whenever the country was in trouble it would call on the sons of New England. The sons of New England would have to take control again if the United States were to survive. Scabb was ready. If Hatch and Jones were indicted, because of that harebrained operation, the Terrible Twos, the party would call upon him to lead. Dean Clift had jumped from two to ten percent in the polls, but this was no problem, and the idea of the D'Roaches presenting some sort of challenge was laughable. The American people were not that stupid. With Nola Payne casting the deciding vote on the side of the New Christian judges, there was no chance that Clift's law suit questioning the legality of his removal from the office would be heard.

"Dear?" Scabb's wife asked, peering at him over the pages of the *Washington Sun,* one eye shut. "What do you make of these rumors about Reverend Jones talking to himself in the Oval Office? I mean, not exactly to himself but to ghosts." She gazed at him out of her watery blue eyes, as he finished his poached egg. She knew more about what was going on inside the White House than he did. She was hooked into a grapevine of domestic servants, who passed on information to their mistresses, who in turn shared the intelligence in beauty salons, and over lunch. "Just gossip, dearest. Reverend Jones is a very spiritual man, perhaps he was praying." Their eyes collided for a moment before careening into their private souls. All they could hear was the scraping of shovels against the concrete as the help cleared the snow that lay before the Veep's garage.

"Kingsley, don't give me that shit. I've heard that he's crazier than Dean was. I also hear that Jesse Hatch is about to be indicted for some kind of land deal. That leaves you." She put down her coffee and squinted at him. She was always running up bills. Always having cosmetic surgery. Her weight was always expanding and contracting. He held the newspaper to one side, for a moment. "What leaves me, hon?"

"Look, Kingsley, don't be coy with me. We've been married for thirty years. I've seen that ambitious look in your eyes for the last three months. Something's cooking, and you know it." John, who worked in the Clift White House, entered the dining room of the Vice Presidential mansion built by Nelson Rockefeller, the butcher of Attica; it was said to be haunted by prisoners and guards wearing convict's clothes and ski masks, and carrying broomsticks.

"Good morning, John. How was your Thanksgiving?"

"Fine, Mr. Vice President, and yours?" John said, pouring more coffee from a silver container.

"Delightful. Nothing like New Hampshire during the Thanksgiving holidays. We all reflect upon that little band of Puritans who—"

"John. Have all of the arrangements for the Xmas party been finalized?" Scabb's wife said, interrupting him. One of her ancestors had been hanged as a witch.

"Yes, Ms. Scabb."

"Good. I'll go over the details with you after breakfast."

"That'll be fine, Ms. Scabb." John had finished pouring the orange juice. He left the dining room. Outside he noticed that nobody was around. He cupped his ear and pinned it to the door of the dining room.

"I never feel comfortable around him. I keep thinking he's comparing me unfavorably with Dean Clift's wife—Kingsley."

"Yes, honey."

"How are we going to be a team when you won't let me know what's going on all of the time? This Operation Two

Birds, for example. People all over town are talking about that Haitian woman's letter. The one written by Admiral Matthews. They're saying that Dean Clift was right. That there was a conspiracy to nuke the cities with huge surplus populations, blame it on Nigeria, and then nuke Nigeria. I don't see why they had to be so sloppy. Why couldn't they have just used ethnic chemicals like crack or heroin or round them all up? I mean that's what this AIDS thing was all about, wasn't it? To get rid of some unpopular groups like faggots and blacks. People who have outlived their usefulness. You could have dumped more crack and heroin into the ghettos. But no, they had to listen to those religious nuts. It was Krantz's idea. He's almost as weird as that Jones. First he was sucking up to Jones, and then Admiral Matthews. Then this Terrible Twos scheme got loose and it's threatening everybody. Can't you get the C.I.A. to do anything right, Kingsley? The stupidest scheme I've ever heard of. If this all gets out, Dean Clift will return to Washington and people will start believing in Santa Claus. You don't know anything about this, do you, Kingsley? It would ruin your career to be involved in such a scandal."

"Who, me? Of course not, dear. President Hatch never tells me anything."

"You'd better not be. Wasn't enough that I caught you at Cardinal Spellman's party with those chorus boys." She began to cry. He had been seen at one of the parties Cardinal Spellman used to throw after the opening of Broadway musicals, but that had been years before. She always managed to bring it up.

John stole away from the door and toward the kitchen, carrying a pitcher of orange juice. He could hear Mrs. Scabb, sobbing in the dining room. The government fired him, as soon as Jesse Hatch and his wife moved into the White House. But when John threatened to write a book about what he'd seen in the White House over the years, they gave him the job of managing the Vice President's household. Esther and Jane still worked at the White House, and they kept him howling as they described the shenanigans going on in the Oval Office since Reverend Jones had taken up residence there. Mrs. Scabb ran past the open door of the kitchen, bawling as she ran to her bedroom. She slammed the door.

7

The turkey was about as gratifying as a Perry Como Xmas carol. The other parts of the menu, giblet gravy, hominy, celery root and spoon bread dressing, roasted chestnut salad, and plum pudding, were about as interesting, but he was hungry and so he dug in.

While Phillip and Virginia stared at each other across the table, sighing and blinking their eyes, he helped himself to the food. He hadn't eaten this well in a long time. Nance finished his meal, and was dabbing at his guardsman's mustache with a Bloomingdale's napkin. Now they were holding each other's hands. Before lapsing into some sort of love trance, they had spent about thirty minutes discussing kiwi and olive oil. Nance cleared his throat. This got Virginia's attention.

"Would you like some coffee, Nance?" she said. Phillip frowned. He had a very narrow face. Little bitty eyes that shifted when you looked into them. He was wearing jeans and black Reeboks. A custom-made shirt and a Brooks Brothers tie. His jacket was designed by Armani. Virginia probably selected Phillip's wardrobe. She was always volunteering to select Nance's when they were married. He always said no thanks. He liked the rumpled look. Once he became attached to an item of clothing, he wouldn't take it off. Sometimes he slept in his favorite shirts and sweaters. These days he was wearing black suits a lot. Virginia told her television audience that her ex-husband was going around dressed like an undertaker. She was always putting down his manners to the delight of the audience. She said that once she introduced him to the great tango accordionist Piazolla, and he said hello Mr. Pia Zadora. She said that he was the type of guy who went into Ethiopian restaurants and requested chopsticks. Virginia was in one of the huge kitchen's alcoves, preparing the coffee. Nance belched. Phillip looked at him with disgust.

"Can I help you with coffee, hon?"

"No, I can handle it, dear," came the answer from the kitchen.

"I hear you received a quarter of a million dollars to write about the surps. Where they are, and where they're going, in which you trace their difficulties to their behavioral patterns. It was in *The Exegesis*," Nance said, a little drunk and looking for trouble.

"Yes. I've already begun my research."

"Now, I agree that some of these surps are their own worst enemies, but you seem to let the government, economics, and racism off the hook. It seems to me that Jesse Hatch's philosophy is that of constructing a two-tier economy in which the surps will take the fall for any fluctuations in the raw market. These people in Washington have already written off millions of these homeless surps, I mean you can't walk down the street without half of the people asking you for five dollars. They got whole families out there begging."

"Those people are crazy. They prefer being out there."

"Crazy? You sound like Pierre DuPont or somebody." It was taking a long time for the coffee to be prepared. In the meantime Nance had knocked down a couple of shots of the rum that Virginia always kept around during the holidays. When they had first married, Virginia had shared his lackadaisical bohemian attitudes toward Xmas, but now she was more enthusiastic than a Jamaican. She had even persuaded the members of the condominium that she lived in to put a manger scene outside.

"Pierre DuPont has a lot of good ideas."

"Yeah, if you and these DuPonts get your way the only people left in this country will be WASPs, the real ones, and the made-in-Taiwan ones like you."

"If WASPs lose power in this country, it will be like killing the goose with the golden egg. Who is going to run the country? You and your surps? Ha. There would be brownouts every thirty minutes, and the telephones wouldn't work," Phillip answered, ignoring Nance's sarcasm.

"And nobody will publish your articles."

"What? What did you say?" Phillip Wheatley was usually very cool, but this last remark got a rise from him.

"Aw, man. They're using you. Every time you write a column, somebody gets kicked off food stamps." Nance was beginning to slur his words.

"Virginia, you'd better come and see about your ex-husband." Virginia brought the tray of coffee into the room, and placed it on the table. "I'm sorry it took so long. I was trying out my new Italian espresso machine. Mr. Whyte gave it to me for Xmas.

"Now, Nance. Are you picking on Phillipkums again?" They both winced. "I think you've had enough of that," she said. She picked up the bottle of rum, clamped a top on it, and placed it on a shelf.

"He was making fun of my column, sugarpie."

"At least you have a job. Nance drifts from job to job. He's almost fifty years old and still hasn't figured out what he wants to do with his time. Whoever named you Nance was right. Anansis. Can't figure out how to grow your yams and potatoes." Nance's grandfather had named him that. He was a professional folklorist. In the old days he just sat around the barbershops telling the old tales. Now he was making eighty thousand a year on the university circuit. "I worked and slaved to help him through law school only to have him conclude one day that there was no such thing as law in America. Only power. He dropped out of law school."

"You'll never let me forget about that, will you?"

"Nance, if you don't know how to act, you can get out of my house. Go back to hustling your fares."

"What?" Phillip said. He had a slight grin. She paused for a moment. She was going to enjoy what she was about to say.

"He drives this old beat-up Cadillac that must have over 200,000 miles on it. It was given to him, or shall I say willed to him by a gangster named Joe Baby. He sneaks around La Guardia, looking for fares, waiting on the Eastern shuttle from Washington. When he has five passengers, he drops them off at hotels downtown. Sometimes he's even able to fit in six. They sit on two seats that pull up from the floor of the backseat." Phillip was really cackling.

"Who was this Joe Baby?" Phillip asked.

"Oh, he was some hoodlum who'd hired a man to do a job for him. The man disappeared. Nance was hired to locate the man. He couldn't because the clues kept getting ahead of him. He was one lousy detective. Now he's driving this car, and helping people avoid bill collectors." They were both laughing now. Nance had his coat on. He belched, an act which really offended them. "He has the manners of Big Jay McNeeley's saxophone with his burps squeals howls and honks. He's always dressing in black these days, like some kind of undertaker. And his stomach. That's his biggest recreation. Filling his stomach. I'll bet that after he leaves here he's going to head to a deli to get a prune danish. His stomach is his only friend. Once while he was asleep I drew a mouth, nose and lips on his stomach. I gave his stomach's face a satisfied look."

Nance had the face of a fat black cat. He stretched his chin out, as he tried to maintain his dignity. He started out of the door, a little tipsy and as they stood there, Phillip's arm around Virginia's waist, Nance couldn't resist one last shot.

"Well, Virginia," he said. "I have to hand it to you. You really scored this time. He must be at least twenty years younger than you are." But she didn't get mad.

"Nance," she said. "You're just mad because he's so sensitive." She ran her hand through his hair. "He's introducing me to new things. He took me to the opera the other night. I'm beginning to enjoy the opera," she said. They were now staring into each other's eyes. "Rigoletto used to drive me crazy." Nance headed downstairs on his way out of the condominium. "He's handsomer than you, smarter than you, and he'll always have more money than you have." Outside Nance stood in the snow for a minute. He looked at his watch. He started to brush the snow off the windows of his car before heading for La Guardia. He stared at the moon for a minute. She's probably right, Nance thought.

8

The origins of Pete and Nick's relationship are unclear. Peter is a Moor, who wound up in a Spanish court, while Nick hails from Turkey, to which, even today, one can travel from Germany via rail. When a legend is imported to another country it often undergoes modification, blending in with and pasting over some local legend. The image of Pete as a gift giver may arise from the popularity of the black King Balthazar figure in European iconography. Nick's size may stem from the black pixy figures from early German mythology, who are depicted on the walls of the Cathedral at Cologne. They are also associated, as Pete is, with switches. There are conflicts as to who does what for and to whom. In many versions of this pair's career, Pete does all of the dirty work, going down chimneys, etc., while Nick poses on a white horse. Though the Turks are dark, Nick becomes pink in the Northern European version, perhaps taking on the appearance of a lost European god. Odin has been suggested. Both perform miracles, and though Nick might intercede on behalf of a commoner, he prefers the geostrategic variety, altering the course of history. Pete works for the persecuted and the down-and-out. He will give you the clothes off his back, but he has a temper and has gotten the reputation for meanness. Having seen so much misery in Northern Europe, he can't even enjoy himself in Guinea, an island underneath the sea, located somewhere in the Caribbean, where twenty-four hours per day carnivals take place, with their samba and salsa societies.

There's a rumor that's been around some hundreds of years that Nick enjoys an erotic fling, and has been known to do orgies. This is the Gnostic Nicholas who is condemned in the Book of Revelations. The eat, drink, and be merry Nicholas, whose style influences the American Xmas, when the waistlines expand and there's carnage on the road caused by intoxicated drivers. His reputation in the ancient world is that of someone equipped with a very active and energetic pelvis. After the trans-Atlantic crossing for the pair, Nick became a part of the American Xmas, but Pete was ignored. Pete is very bitter about this, and spends time in his apartment in Guinea, being bitter. Of course, Nick's appearance in the American Xmas wasn't all that flattering either. His bad body image in a place where weight watching is the national "mania," as Carson McCullers would say. But, unlike Peter, at least he was visible. Even in Guinea where he had a following his image didn't please him. An apelike creature climbing up and down ropes in Dutch department stores. He wants respect. He wants his propers. He had been cheated out of history. If they only knew that Nick received credit that rightly belonged to him, maybe Americans would leave out soup for him. Maybe he'd be invited to join the Macy's Thanksgiving Day parade.

He could hear the groups outside, the Delta music from Martinique and Zairian rhumba, the stands set up along the way hawking the kind of food they ate in Kinshasa, New Orleans, Guadalupe, Peytonville, and Fort-de-France. They ate Navajo Tacos and Buffalo Burgers. They drank strong fruited drinks.

Black Peter was still moody. He couldn't enjoy himself. He didn't like the way he went out. He was like Larry Holmes. He didn't feel that he'd received his credit. Holmes was the champ, yet it was Gerry Cooney's face that made *Time*. He beat Mike Spinks twice, but was robbed. During Christmas he got the big SAD. Seasonal Affective Disorder. There was a knock at the door. It was Nescafe, who spent most of his time poking around for available uteruses and playing piccolo or gazing at nipples and crotches. He wore sandals, and his toes were covered with sand. He wore a brown and white cotton smock, and black pants, and on his head he wore a fez. Underneath his eyes were three parallel, horizontal white lines, covering his skin as brown as Swiss instant coffee. His facial features were simian, like those of the early cartoons on Paddy, the stereotypical Irishman. As soon as he entered Pete's apartment, his eyes began nosing around, picking up on this or that item. "Just thought I'd stop by since I was in the neighborhood," he said. He was the type who never merely stopped by because he was in the neighborhood.

"Man, you sit up here in this apartment, lights out, dressed in black. You never go out unless it's to cheat some poor devil out of his soul." There were bookshelves lined with ancient and leather-bound books bearing Northern European titles: *The Meaning of Meaning, Vol. Twenty-three.* The room's furniture was also of the same national mixture. The refrigerator was always full of Dutch schnapps and seafood. Peter liked spicy foods and white chocolate.

"You're upset because the Americans don't recognize you.

They recognize Nick. So even though we have all of this good music, food, women, white rum, dancing, carnival twenty-four hours a day, you're unhappy. That's because you spent all of that time in Northern Europe. Those winters, and twenty-four-hour days. The long nights, and the restless dead. Taking an African and putting him in one of those places is like trying to domesticate a white shark. Something dies within the African soul, or he gets a Ph.D., which is the intellectual equivalent of a lobotomy. While you're up here doing your Kierkegaard bit, some guy in New York is partying away at the expense of your reputation." Black Peter lunged at Nescafe, and within seconds had him pinned to the floor. Struggling for air and gasping, Nescafe protested. "Get off of me. Stop choking me." Black Peter let him go. Nescafe brushed himself off. "You have a mean and nasty temper, Peter. That's why you're slowly being banished from history. Whipping children, going down the chimney for white people. You'll never be as loved and as admired as Saint Nicholas."

"You have to tell me about this imposter."

"I'll think about it."

"What do you mean, you'll think about it?"

"There's this Caribbean queen I ran into down at the beach. You mix me some of that Love Powder, so that she will find me irresistible. For this I'll give you the information."

"I don't do that kind of stuff anymore. I'm more into thought, Creative Visualization. Positive transmission. That sort of thing."

"I'm trying to get laid, and you're talking this Northern European nonsense. OK. I'll keep the information to myself." Nescafe got up to leave.

"Hold on, Nescafe. I'll give you the stuff." He went to a cabinet and brought down a small oval-shaped box of Love Powder. It looked like paprika, guaranteed to make a man irresistible to a woman. Nescafe slipped it into his pocket. "OK, give me the goods," Pete said.

"I'd like a bottle of Dutch schnapps first." After Pete gave Nescafe a bottle of schnapps, Nescafe told him the strange story of the Terrible Twos Xmas, about a Forty-second Street hustler who owned a bizarre act using an almost human dummy, until somebody stole his dummy and he got in with Boy Bishop and his gang, who were devoted to a noncommercial Xmas. Picketing toy exhibits and conferences, and making things miserable for the multibillion-dollar Xmas industry. He told him about Big North, the North Pole Development Corporation, which bought the exclusive rights to Santa Claus, therefore driving all of the Santas out of business. He told him about how Boy Bishop stole prostitutes from pimps because this was one of Nick's stunts, that of rescuing maidens from prostitution. He told of how this got Boy Bishop in trouble with Joe Baby and Big Meat, two gangsters, and how they sent Snow Man, a white hood, to ice Boy Bishop, and how Bishop and Peter and his cohorts were able to kill Snow Man and use the fat gangster's corpse as a Xmas zombie, through which Peter the ventriloquist would pipe all sorts of socialistic speeches against the exploitation of Xmas by merchants. He talked about how Pete took over the Nicolaites and threw a big non-traditional Xmas party at Madison Square Garden which goons, acting on behalf of Big North in league with the Xmas merchants, broke up, and how this riot had sent Pete and his followers into the underground. He told him how a calypso song had brought Pete back into prominence, and how Jack Frost, one of his former enemies, had recruited him to work for the toy manufacturers who knew a good merchandising stunt when they saw one. He told Pete how Pete, the impostor, was living off his name, on a whole floor of suites for his followers and for himself, and how they were having a grand time partying every night and devoting themselves to pleasure. Looking about Pete's place, Nescafe said, "He has a bedroom that makes this place seem modest, a big bed with a canopy hanging over it, with a constant procession of women — show dancers and actresses. All because he's cashing in on your identity. Boy, if he were doing that to me, I'd be real sore." Black Peter was depressed. He put his head into his hands.

"All of these years I've tried to clear my name. Now I'm not only a boogeyman and a clown in Europe, but a fool in America."

"That's about the truth," Nescafe said, smiling.

Nescafe got up to leave. "Thanks for the love potion, Pete. If I hear anything else I'll let you know. I'll keep my ears open." Pete was raging inside.

"Did you hear what I said?"

He looked up at Nescafe.

"I said I'd keep my ears open."

"You won't have to. I'm going to New York," Pete said. Disguised as a snowstorm, Pete landed in New York.

9

Dean Clift was in his robe, his hands behind his back, pacing back and forth, biting on a cigar. Robert Marshal, his aide, had brought him the news of the events transpiring in Washington. The rumors that Reverend Jones was not acting rationally. The strange and sudden death of Admiral Matthews. Bob Krantz's disappearance. The letter that had been sold to Pedigree by Admiral Matthews's maid, revealing that there had been such a thing as Operation Two Birds. The lights in the White House were burning all night as they tried to decide what to do. The progress of his suit against Jesse Hatch's administration would soon be argued before the Supreme Court.

"This is the best news we've gotten in three years, and you don't seem too happy, Bob?"

"Look, even if it turns out that you were telling the truth, they can still get you on that Nicholas business. How do we deal with that?"

"But it's true. What about the others? There were others who said that Nicholas came to them."

"Oh, they were seen as imitators. You know, once you

get the reputation in Washington that you're weird, it's hard to straighten it out. After Goldwater said he believed in flying saucers, his credibility plummeted. Besides, with Nola Payne casting the swing vote on the court, siding with the New Christian judges, you don't have a chance."

"I don't think that we should give up. I still have a loyal following. They tell me that there are always crowds outside the gates of this place. My people will stand by me."

"I hope you're right."

"How's the race for next year shaping up?"

"They're talking about putting Hatch up, but there's a rumor going around town that Jones is fed up with Hatch. Kingsley Scabb is organizing his blue-blood buddies for a shot at the White House, but he doesn't have a chance unless he can get the backing of Jones's operation. Those people are the most organized political movement in American history. My god, they get your telephone number and you might as well forget it. I've had mine changed four times. You see what happened to those televangelists who stood in Jones's way? He Matthewed every one of them. Most of them are on relief, or living in trailers. Some were fortunate enough to get modest congregations. Others went to jail for stealing donations. As chief of staff, he was able to put them under surveillance. I mean, they were bound to come up with something. Everybody has something to hide. When the F.B.I. sent Jones the Hoover files, he stayed in the Oval Office for four weeks with a Do Not Disturb sign on the doorknob.

"A real crazy man."

"Why did you let him put you on the ticket under General Scott?"

"Who could have known that the guy believed all of that

stuff? The thing about Jews and blacks being children of the
devil. The premillenarianism. Look, I didn't want to end
up—it's sad what happens to old models, you're lucky if you
can get a commercial spot pushing over-fifty life insurance.
I just felt that a political career would be a way to gain a
little prestige and travel, go to parties. I mean, I was a pretty
superficial guy, and the money that backed me insisted that
I push the—well, you know there were these black guys in
Air Jordans and hoods who were terrorizing New York, and
the welfare hotels, and the teenage pregnancies—I was drinking a lot, because I never had anything against blacks. But
I had to get elected, and then when they offered me the spot
on the Scott ticket, I thought, what a soft job. Breaking ties
in the Senate, going to funerals—but then Scott died, and
I really went off the deep end."

"Yeah, meeting with the head of the Nazi party in the
White House, and awarding Bernhard Goetz the Medal of
Freedom; I'll say you did, and then proposing that the capital
be moved to Cicero, Illinois, a town that you said exemplified
the values and traditions of Western civilization. And then
that proposal of yours to declare Adolph Hitler's birth date a
national holiday—"

"I never went that far, that was leaked from someone within
the administration, but—I guess I was pretty far gone, but
then Elizabeth's death. Her electrocution while lighting the
Christmas tree. And then the experience. Nicholas. Those
kinds of things change a man."

"You sure did change. I never will forget that speech. I
was sitting there watching the football game with some friends
at Cape Cod, and the game was interrupted by your speech.
You revealed that covert operation, the Terrible Twos. We
couldn't believe it. After your speech nobody in the room

spoke. We thought that the country deserved a rest after all of the Terribles. And here was another Terrible. With more indictments. Hearings. Witnesses. Special prosecutors. And when they sent you here we believed them. The story they gave out that you were seeing things that weren't there. That you were acting bizarrely. We wanted to believe it."

"So why did you come down here? You've been working here for three years without pay."

"Because, I don't know, it's maybe you remind me of my youth, when there was such a thing as Santa Claus. When we believed that America could be a place for everybody, regardless of race, creed or color—you know, all of the things we learned in high school during the fifties, those civics classes. Some of us believed in all of that, but then J.F.K. killed, Nixon, Reagan, we seemed to become more and more cynical, more and more jaded, the music, the art, the buck became the bottom line in everything. And so when you made that speech, those of us who hated your guts began to cheer you."

Dean walked to the window, and stared through the bars which were misshapen by the snow. "I was just along for the ride. I didn't care about what Reverend Jones was up to. But after Elizabeth, and Nicholas, after those experiences, I changed. If I ever get out of here, I'm going to straighten things out."

"They'll never let you out. You're dangerous. Reverend Jones plans to keep you here as long as he can. People inside this place are from the secret government. The army is down at the gates. Something's got to be done, though. The allies are getting nervous. This thing Jones has about premilleni-arianism. He might push the button. He might think that we're all better off in heaven."

10

I should be sitting in that chair. This man is as crazy and unpredictable as a baby black panther. Wait until the press discovers what he does with his time. Talks to some ghost whom he says is the spirit of a departed S.S. officer, who stowed away on Air Force 1 when Reagan returned from laying the wreath at Bitburg. Supposed to sit in that empty chair, dressed in the Bavarian national costume. A superhero they lent him from Hollywood, Joe Beowulf. He sends his computer generated fantasy out to snuff his enemies. Oh, uh. It's staring at me. I wonder can it read thoughts. I'll just play along until next year. Don't want to alienate these New Christians. The best campaigners in the history of the country. Everybody's got their phones off the hook, they're such pests. Used to dismiss them, until that miracle they performed in the early part of this decade, electing General Walter Scott, the hero of Dominica. I wasn't surprised when he died. He was swaying and staggering about during the inaugural ceremony. And that invasion of Dominica. Just a stunt. Word has it that Hollywood paid for it. They only found one communist in the whole country, and he turned out to be a C.I.A. plant and

*the prime minister claims she never invited U.S. troops in like
the administration claimed. Then Dean Clift. Feel kind of
sorry about the guy. Talked about seeing Saint
Nicholas. Weirder things have happened around here. My
wife tells me that one of the White House maids opened the
door of a room one night and saw Edith Wilson nagging her
paralyzed husband. And Jesse Hatch. Reverend Jones has
taken over so as White House chief of staff that nobody rec-
ognizes Jesse Hatch on the street. Just a figurehead, posing
with turkeys. Word has it that Jones has the goods on Jesse
Hatch. Some kind of land deal and a bribe. And then these
maniacs, the D'Roaches, getting on the ballot. People who
believe that salad bars are part of a communist conspiracy.
That eggs ain't poultry, grits ain't groceries, and Mona Lisa
was a man. The only thing that's gonna rescue this country
from the endless Terribles is for the Sons of New England to
take control again.*

"What's your opinion, Scabb?"

"Opinion?"

"Goddamnit, Scabb, pay attention. I was telling Heinrich
and Joe here why I had to get rid of that Heeb, Krantz. You
know this thing that Dean Clift was babbling about? Well,
part of the story is true. Without the knowledge of Matthews,
the King of Beer, and me, Krantz had gotten involved in
some lone cowboy scheme to use nuclear weapons against
Miami and New York, and then blame it on Nigeria. He
was the point man for an international network for reasons
we're still investigating. I think that he might be some kind
of Zionist agent, you know like Pollard, back there in the
eighties." He examined Scabb closely to see whether the story
that he and Hatch had hatched would take.

So they're going to make Krantz the fall guy, huh? Scabb

thought. "Why, I'm shocked to hear that, Mr. Prez—I mean, Reverend," Scabb said. "He was a likable young man."

"I don't think that this will affect the court case with Clift. We can say that he was right about Krantz, and that we didn't know anything about it, but this experience he was supposed to have had about Saint Nicholas ought to keep him in Buggy Bye for years to come. What's wrong, Scabb?"

"I need a glass of water. This is such a shock. I . . . ." Scabb had done some theater in college and so he seemed to be very convincing to Jones. Jones nodded toward Beowulf. The machine got up and went to a table. Poured water from a pitcher into a glass. Brought it over to Scabb. Shoved it into Scabb's hand. Scabb said thanks, trembling. *When I'm elected the first thing I'm going to do is to take a hammer and break that thing up. Keep the Viking helmet and battle-ax though. Might look good in the living room, Scabb thought. And that bear fur he uses for shorts. Could use that on the floor of one of the upstairs bathrooms.* "I mean, Krantz. He was such a nice young man. And you mean to tell me that he was involved in some kind of off-the-shelf operation?"

"I'm afraid so. You must know how it hurts me. I brought him into the administration. It was I who rescued him from a close call with death. And so I bear the responsibility. I'll have to take care of it. Me, Joe, and Heinrich, here," Jones said, nodding toward the empty chair, where, for Reverend Jones, his advisor Heinrich sat.

"Of course, Reverend Jones," Scabb said, glancing toward the empty chair.

"I'm glad you agree, Scabb. You keep remaining loyal to me and you may be rewarded. Iowa is only around the corner and that straw poll will be taking place soon. I would run myself but the media has always been against me."

Bad enough that he said he'd had personal experiences with Satan, but if they knew about his new thing, Beowulf and Heinrich, they'd put him out where they put Clift, Scabb thought.

"You know, after Clift was dealt with, I mentioned in an interview that I would run, and the media, agents of the archfiend, began to dig into my record and distort passages from my sermons. All the fuss they made about my account of a discussion with Satan that I once had."

And that wasn't all, Scabb thought.

"We New Christians have millions of votes at our disposal, and our people are known to have the reputation for going from door to door, at all times of the day and night, worrying people for their votes. And if they don't open the door, we get their telephone numbers and put our computers to work, harassing them, and wearing them down. We are relentless. Besides, I'm beginning to enjoy this job as chief of staff. I'll be available for the job when you're elected, Scabb."

"Why, of course, Reverend Jones. I'd want you to stay. That is, if you would consider my candidacy. I certainly couldn't bring it off without the support of the New Christians. But what about Hatch?"

"The guy is losing his grip. He may be retiring soon. The ticker," Reverend Jones said, pointing to his chest. Scabb could hardly restrain his glee. Sure he'd promised Reverend Jones that he could stay on as chief of staff, but, hell, in politics promises were made to be broken.

"Heinrich, Joe, and I want to be alone, so Vice President Scabb, if you will excuse us." The drums started up again. They were coming from somewhere deep inside of the city. They both heard, but ignored them. The Vice President started toward the exit, but somehow found himself in the Rose Garden. There was a lot of commotion and laughter. A crunching sound. President Hatch was rolling on the ground, and a Thanksgiving turkey was hopping on his chest. The turkey's feathers were flying.

11

Jack Frost gazed admiringly at Elder Marse's collection of oriental sculpture and furniture. Mr. Marse had hired a security guard from Carson Richard's firm to guard the prize, worth over ten million dollars. The guard stood outside of the door. Elder Marse, billionaire toyman, had many millions left over, even after paying the government's fifty million dollar fine for a Wall Street crime. His office was located inside of a many-storied mid-Manhattan skyscraper. The protesters who'd complained that such a building would block out the sun were overruled by the courts. Below, in the streets, the thousands of homeless were scrounging about in the shadows, pushing grocery carts containing all of their belongings.

Marse had filed Chapter Eleven during Xmas four years before, the Xmas of the Terrible Twos, when demonstrations drastically curbed the Xmas sales; there had always been a noncommercial Xmas movement but the antics of the Nicolaites and the inflammatory media speeches of Black Peter had exacerbated the situation. Elder Marse had bounced back from the Xmas Crash of the T.T.'s, and was now managing this middle-90s Xmas before surrendering to serve six months at a California federal prison, nicknamed "Club Fed" by insiders, for an insider-trading scam that had wiped out hundreds of investors. He had chosen his own jail, and was given a suite of cells, equipped with ten telephones, computers, a chef, a masseuse, and two color television sets. For a couple of Heath bars and some heavy metal records Santa Barbara surfing blondes would come down and administer to his needs all night, or take a cruise on one of his yachts, while the bribed guards looked the other way. Jack Frost was the only man on Big North's payroll to survive the scandal of the Terrible Twos and was now working for Elder Marse as a floorwalker or troubleshooter. His old boss, Ozwald Zumwalt—an alias, he'd run across the name in Jane's fighting ships—was living in Florida. Two other survivors were also living in Florida, Vixen and her husband Stuart, who had been hired by Big North to play Santa Claus, only to be kidnapped by Black Peter and the gang and replaced with a dummy, the corpse of the gangster Snow Man. Vixen still hadn't recovered her speech after discovering Black Peter feeding the corpse of Snow Man with the drops of Tarpon Springs water, supposedly the tears of the original Saint Nicholas. Bro Andrew, the red-haired white dred who had been introduced to Rastafarianism by Black Peter, had abandoned the impostor and taken up residence in the Santa Cruz mountains. Their roosters, dogs, and goats disturbed their neighbors.

Jack Frost enjoyed free-lancing. He made his own hours. And Elder Marse only called on him when he needed to apply a little extra persuasion to a stubborn client. Jack and

Elder Marse were talking quietly between sips of sherry. Marse was seated in a made-in-Korea antique chair with a dragon on its back.

"Jack, I've grown fond of you in the past few years." Elder Marse wore a blue striped shirt, red suspenders and a flowing bow tie. His chin looked as though it were expecting. He was bald, and wore a black patch over one eye. "My colleagues and I won't forget that you were the only one remaining to deal with that Nicolaite band when they tried to keep the consumers from our stores. You've done a lot of good work for me."

"Why thanks, Elder Marse," Jack said, leaning toward the toyman, one hand on a hip, the other holding his empty glass.

"Don't mention it, Jack. Here, have some more sherry." Jack poured from a decanter that was a remnant of one of the important Chinese dynasties.

"We've bounded back in four years, but with these endless Terribles, the stock market crash, and what have you, our sales are still pretty spotty."

"I know, Mr. Marse." Since coming on board Elder Marse's organization, Jack had taken to reading the *Wall Street Journal*.

"Our sales are only marginally above those of last year. We need something dramatic. Something that will give us a big push." Elder Marse gazed at Jack. He was meditative.

"What do you propose, Mr. Marse?"

"Jack, I've been reading the newspapers about this Black Peter phenomenon. Wasn't he one of the leaders of the Xmas boycott during the Xmas of the Terrible Twos? Why, this record hit has been at the top of the chart for almost six months now. Look at this." Elder Marse placed some clipped newspaper ads before Jack. They showed all of the Black Peter products. The Black Peter doll was outselling the Cabbage Patch doll of the 80s.

"This Black Peter is bigger than Michael Jackson. Why, during the intermission of football games, crowds are shouting Black Peter, Jack. I think this Black Peter is just the thing that we need to put into the cash register. And just think, it was only a few years ago that the public was screaming for his skin, after that playboy Boy Bishop, that hippie, revealed how Black Peter took over his group and forced him out."

"What are you getting at, Mr. Marse?"

"Jack, I'm a businessman. I know that you're a little upset with Black Peter after what happened at the garden during the T.T.'s, but money doesn't give a rat's ass about who makes it. Look at that Reagan fellow back there in the eighties. Anticommunist for years. His anticommunism was preventing us from making a dollar in one of the biggest markets in the world. The Soviet Union. So we told the son of a bitch that if he didn't soften his attitude and sign that treaty with them back there in the 1980s that he and Nancy would have to spend their retirement years doing commercials. We threatened to take away that big house in California and refuse to contribute to his library. Now this crazy crowd in Washington is calling him a left-winger. What I'm trying to tell you Jack is that you have to put aside your personal feud with Black Peter for the sake of the industry. We earn a quarter of our sales during December. Xmas is our tent pole season. The other eleven months merely serve as a warm-up. We need Black Peter to pump sales. Electronic toys aren't faring well. People are squawking about war toys, sexist toys, you name it. We need something with which to build consumer confidence. That's what it's all about. Jack, I want you to find this Black Peter. Make him a deal. We'll provide the guy with luxuries he's never experienced before. I checked his background. He grew up on the Lower East Side in those projects on Avenue D. First got arrested for stealing a Xmas ham. A bunch of auto thefts, a drug arrest, and then he ran a con game with a dummy down in midtown. So it shouldn't take much. He's not used to anything. A Cadillac, a Minnesota Viking, and a discount suite at our hotel ought to do it. We'll give him some spending money. Maybe $100,000. Pocket money to me."

"Now wait a minute, Mr. Marse. You're asking me to bring in Black Peter?"

"Black Peter is already in. I want you to find him. Get him to work for us."

"I don't know, Mr. Marse."

"Look, Jack. I'm going to be away for six months. Maybe three months for good behavior. I need somebody to kind of keep an eye on things while I'm gone. Somebody I can trust. Case anybody gets ideas about a hostile takeover or something." Jack Frost, a man so cold that he went to a musical on the day of his grandmother's funeral, wasn't the brightest guy but he was bright enough.

"I'll bring him to you, tomorrow, Mr. Marse."

"I knew that I could count on you, Jack." Mr. Marse rose from the chair behind the desk. He went over and put his arm around Jack, and escorted him out of his office.

12

The phony Black Peter—wanted by every city, state, and
federal law enforcement agency that you could give letters of
the alphabet to—was struggling for survival in a cave underneath Manhattan, since the Madison Square Garden Xmas
riots. He and his followers were always being set upon by
desperate surps, who were robbing them and stealing the food
that some of Peter's followers scavenged from the garbage
bins of supermarkets. Most of the white dreds who'd followed
him had returned to their suburbs, after polite, middle-class
plea bargaining. Many had moved on to prep school or joined
Reverend Jones's Christian majority, which was signing up
students by droves on the campuses. The remaining ones
had become fed up with the squalid life and were getting on
one another's nerves. Black Peter's British accent had become
even more affected, and he'd become a pill to live around.
He spent his time sending his followers out to steal for him,
or smoking Philadelphia marijuana and recovering from the
headaches. One of his followers had died mixing Philadelphia and New York grass. He had the reggae music turned
up loud, or spent hours manipulating his dreds, which were

dirty and entangled. He always talked about the dreds as being the appendage of his manhood, and that cutting them off would be like cutting off his manhood.

The next-to-last one to leave was Freddie King Jr., and he would have remained had not State Senator King, the most dapper legislator ever to hit Albany, sent a debriefer after him. Mysteriously, his father had resigned from the Senate a year later. Peter cried when he buried Snow Man's corpse. He had become fond of the dummy. But Tarpon Springs, the outfit that sent Peter the tears of Saint Nicholas, the solution that kept the zombie alive, had gone out of business. But even his severest critics commented about what they called Black Peter's rescuing, his ability to rise to the occasion, or rather, his charmed life, and so just as it seemed that he was done for, a calypso song that chronicled Xmas of four years before, the Terrible Twos, became a hit. It was all about Black Peter and his adventures. So just as he was about to leave the cave, his resources having been exhausted, to return to his old panhandling spot in midtown, he was greeted by a visitor who was standing near a stack of blankets, and a dying fire which was keeping him warm. He recognized the man immediately. He was dressed in a cashmere overcoat, and was wearing a white scarf. He still had that sharp profile which had the contours of an ax.

"Look, I don't want any trouble."

"I'm not here to give you any," Jack Frost said, squatting near where Black Peter sat, his earphones tuned into Peter Tosh, on a pile of dirty blankets in a long, dirty box.

"I know that you're probably offended by the calamitous events of Xmas, the Terrible Twos Xmas, but that Madison Square caper wasn't my fault. It was Boy Bishop, and those, those rich and privileged cohorts, they put me up to it, they were into black magic, they used the living corpse of a gangster . . . I . . . I . . . I had no choice—"

"Look, pal. I don't blame you for what happened. Both of us were being used by others. I was being used by the North Pole Development Corporation, you were used by those rejects from Newport."

"You really mean that? You're not sore?"

"Being sore is counterproductive. Why should I hold a grudge when there's money to be made?"

"I don't understand."

"What, you haven't heard?"

"Heard what?"

"They got a song out about you that's been at the top of the record hits for about thirteen weeks now. You're a hero."

"A hero? Me, a hero?"

"Sure, everybody is singing the Black Peter song. How you defied the toy manufacturers. It's got a social protest angle, but that doesn't seem to be any problem. Why, last week Jesse Hatch said he was buying an album for his children."

"What?"

"Sure. Look at this." Jack Frost showed him full-page ads and clippings about the huge sales programs that were being mounted, exploiting his image. There were Black Peter dolls, Black Peter bicycles, Black Peter wine, Black Peter perfumes, Black Peter pennants, and even something called the Black Peter look. There was a rap group called the Black Peters. Black Peter was stunned. He had been the public's goat for four years, ever since the Madison Square Garden riots, and now he was on the rise again. Proving once again that the raw market values of capitalism were chaotic.

"I'd like to be your agent."

"Agent, agent for what?"

"I got some toy manufacturers, Xmas card producers, and others waiting downtown to see you. But first we got to get you cleaned up."

"What do you mean?"

"Those dreds. We think that you ought to get them cut. Your image should be a little more crossover."

"No way, I can't part with my dreds. To part with my dreds would be to part with my manhood."

"Suit yourself," Jack Frost said, rising and blowing over his black-gloved hand.

"They were talking about giving you a hefty advance for your services." Jack Frost turned around and was about to exit from the cave. "A golden Rolls Royce with zebra skin interior, and a Minnesota Viking to ride around with. All you have to do is feed her a steady supply of Baby Ruths to keep her happy."

"Wait. Wait. I'm willing to reason all of this out," Black Peter said. "I'm a reasonable person." Jack Frost, his back to Black Peter, smiled. He turned around. Walked toward Black Peter and extended his hand. Black Peter took hold of it and stood up. Black Peter was cleaned up, was taken downtown where he was given two hundred hours community service for his role in the disturbances at Madison Square Garden, and was driven to the hotel for his meeting with captains of the Xmas industry, in a sports car especially designed for him, called the Petermobile. His fans were faked out as a decoy Petermobile drove up to the front of the hotel. His employees didn't want his fans to see him until after his appointment with the plastic surgeon.

13

Bob Krantz, director of White House communications, got as far as the White House gates, only to be told that he wouldn't be admitted. "President's orders," the guard had said, but he knew this to be a lie. Everybody knew that Hatch had no power to give anybody orders. Krantz returned to his Georgetown apartment and had Eric, his valet, mix him a stiff highball. He had grown accustomed to the place where he was living and enjoyed its customs. That afternoon he read James Way, a Jiminy Cricket–headed columnist who wore bow ties and a head of hair which was greased like that of Alfalfa of "Our Gang" fame. He couldn't get through a column without quoting at least three dead Greeks. Way, who was Reverend Jones's mouthpiece in the press, said that Krantz was resigning to take an ambassadorial post, and had been hailed by Jesse Hatch as a true public servant. Krantz knew that Way was always over at the White House sucking up the sewer for information, but couldn't believe that Reverend Jones, his former mentor, would be so cold. It had to be underlings. If only he could get to Jones. Jones would stop the whole thing. Sure, they weren't as close as they were at one time, but he knew that Reverend Jones had high regard for him. Besides, it was important that he had befriended Admiral Matthews, because Matthews was an authority on the nuclear Navy. He had to find out how the remaining weapons functioned. There wasn't much time left. But the Way revelations were serious. Krantz knew then that he was slated to be blocked and removed. This was the same story that was put out when the string quartet loving Secretary of Defense had been killed. Of course they'd said that it was a suicide, but that didn't sail because Krantz was in on the meeting when Admiral Matthews, Reverend Jones, and the King of Beer decided that the Secretary of Defense had been marked. They were all afraid that he'd reveal the Terrible Twos. Were they planning to do the same to him? He hadn't made such a long journey just to be somebody's fall guy. He had other plans. Reverend Jones was really deteriorating. He was remaining in the Oval Office. He wouldn't let anybody clean in there, and he'd wash his underwear and his socks, and hang them from a line strung across the room. He hadn't been home in weeks. Everybody was concerned about his appearance at Admiral Matthews's funeral, but he had, some-how, brought it off. Eric packed some clothes, went to the bank and withdrew some money. He returned and gave it to Krantz. He didn't know what he'd do without Eric. Some of his friends told him to never trust a gentile, but he didn't know what they were talking about. They thought that he was Jewish. The name. He never said anything about it, and when they tried to get familiar he always had an excuse. He would say that he was an American. He got on the shuttle and headed for New York. As soon as he left, Eric, his valet, called the White House and apprised them of Krantz's move.

14

Fryer Moog called the bank only to discover that he had bounced thirteen checks. His charge cards, all three hundred of them, were over the limit, and carrying forty percent interest. The cook, chauffeur, and maids had quit. His wife had left him. He looked up at the mantelpiece and noticed that the Grammies, Emmies, and Oscars had been pawned. The living room was a mess, and his nose was bleeding and he didn't know why. Balls of bloody tissue were everywhere. He felt as though chiggers were crawling over him, and he began to scratch himself, vigorously. He rose from the dirty blankets, where he'd been lying for about a week, and tramped through the boxes of pizza which were crawling with flies. His wet pajamas clung to his skin. He went to the window and stared down at his five cars. The cars weren't there. They had been repossessed. It almost took him a half hour to reach the bottom of the circular staircase, he was so thin and weak. He went outside to check the mailbox. Bills. The bank was threatening to put his home in foreclosure. But he didn't care about the bills, his wife, the furniture being repossessed, all he cared about was getting some more coke. He thought for a while. That's it. He'd make a new album with his meal ticket, Boy Junior. Boy Junior's albums sold by the millions. And after that they could do a tour. All he'd have to do would be to get Boy Junior's manager to OK the deal, and he could begin composing the music, which shouldn't take more than a couple of days to organize.

15

A man was half running toward Nance's car. He had emerged from the shuttle terminal and was agitated. He kept looking over his shoulder. The man got into his car.

"Where to?" Nance asked the man.

The man gave Nance a Greenwich Village address. "Please hurry." He was short of breath, and underneath his overcoat Nance could see a pin-striped suit and a striped tie.

"I have to wait for some more passengers, I—" The man shoved a fistful of bills into Nance's hand. *A few more customers like this guy and Big Meat, I can pay down on another limousine and get some guy to work for me,* Nance thought.

When they arrived at the Greenwich Village address, the man started to get out of the car, when they both noticed another man, or rather a creature, standing across the street, his muscles bulging under an overcoat. He was built like Arnold Schwarzenneger, and had Mike Tyson's thick neck. He started for the limousine. "Lock the door," Nance's passenger said. The creature moved across the street as if in slow motion, and when he reached the car he began to bang on the windows. To Nance, he looked as though he were dressed for Halloween. He wore one of those horned Viking helmets over blond hair tied in pigtails. His mustache and beard were also blond. He was bare down to his waist. His middle was covered with what appeared to be bear skin. He wore boots tied in a zigzag pattern.

"We got to get out of here," the man said.

"Holy shit," Nance said. He started up the engine and began to move, but the Hercules merely grabbed hold of the car's rear. Nance accelerated the machine, but it wouldn't move, its wheels spun. Finally, the creature fell back and Nance sent the car spinning around the corner. The creature began running toward them, but soon disappeared from sight.

"Hey," Nance finally said. "I know you. I saw your photo in the newspaper. You're Bob Krantz, advisor to President Jesse Hatch, you said that blacks couldn't accept Victorian values because their genes were bad." Nance stopped the car. "Get the fuck out of my car. And I don't want your money."

"But, but. They'll kill me. I don't have anywhere to go." There was no time for conversation, because heading toward them was the creature, Joe Beowulf, driving a red Triumph. Nance swerved out of the way and headed uptown, tearing through traffic.

"What do we do now?"

"That's your problem, buddy, I don't want to get mixed up in this jam you've gotten yourself into." Bob Krantz put a thousand-dollar bill into the tray that was built into the window separating the back and the front seats. Nance took a long take of the money.

"I'll put you up in my place until we can lose this guy." They drove uptown, and Nance, who knew Manhattan like a spider knows his web, finally lost the creature.

16

Big Mike and the boys were sitting around, playing cards in the back room of Acme Records. The walls in the lobby were covered with gold records their artists had won. They were talking about how some of the younger members of the "organization" didn't have "no" respect, and how one of them had come up to Big Mike and called him by that name, the name that had been reserved for only some of his "executives." "I tried to keep him in the lobby, boss, but the guy pushed me out of the way," Mike's "secretary" said. "It's OK," Big Mike said, chewing on a cigar stub and not lifting his head from the cards. When the other fellas saw that Mike wasn't bothered, they and the secretary put away their "toys."

"What's on your mind, Moog?" Mike said.

"You got a lotta nerve busting in here like this," one of Mike's assistants said. Mike looked over at the assistant, who was furious, and calmed him with his eyes. He then focused on Moog, and Moog could tell that he was annoyed, but Moog didn't care. He was standing there scratching himself; he smelled as though his clothes had been cleaned by cheap chemicals.

"Mike, I'll come to the point, I . . . I need some cash. I thought we'd get Boy Junior to make another album, you know, like the last one, we sold thirty million copies. Mike. Man, these people are threatening to put a foreclosure on my house, and I . . ." Moog nodded for a moment, shut his eyes. He began to reel. And scratch himself. He then awoke. "Mike, O shit, I forgot what I came up here for." The guys who were sitting with Mike, playing a hand of cards, began to look at each other and smile.

"You were saying that you needed some cash. What the fuck do you want me to do, spade?"

"Motherfucker, I'm the one who brought Boy Junior up here. Man, I was the one who sold him to you. Shit, you've made millions of dollars off of his ass." Moog was screaming. The shit was all in his bloodstream and brain cells, and he felt bold and confident.

"But what about the money you owe me?"

"Get lost nigger, you've been coming up here for three weeks asking me the same thing." Moog thought for a minute.

"I have?" The men laughed. The laughter was derisive, mocking.

"Well, pay me then."

"Fuck you, Moog. You snorted and free based all of your profits."

"But, but you said that the shit, and the pills, and the dope, and all—you said—I thought you were giving me that shit to get me to . . . to do my arrangements better." The men laughed again.

"You said you didn't want cash, you wanted cowboy. That's what you said, didn't he, boys?" Mike said. The men nodded, and laughed again.

"You got a lot of nerve calling yourself a composer. Every musician in Hollywood has got a plagiarism suit against you for stealing their shit," Mike said, turning serious for a moment.

"Those people are just jealous. Jealous of my genius. Look, Big Mike, you're managing Boy Junior. Get him to come down from that multimillion-dollar tree house and record another record. I should be finished with the songs tomorrow if I work all night, and I can get what's-his-name to throw together some of that hooker choreography and we'll go in and do a video and, before you know it—"

"We don't need you, nor that nigger dancer anymore."

"What are you talking about?"

"Don't you remember?"

"Remember what?"

"You came in here the day before yesterday and sold us that synthesizer that composes all of your music. You know, the one that you had that Jap make for you. We don't need you anymore. Don't you remember? You started crying, didn't he, boys? Said that you were desperate for some more shit."

"I did?" The men broke up. "Wait until Boy Junior hears about this. He needs me. He won't stand for it. Where is he?" Fryer said, trying to make himself heard over the laughter.

"He got in his jet and flew to Greece because he heard that there was a sighting of a unicorn. You know, he's been searching all over the world for a unicorn. Craziest spade I ever met, but the motherfucker is like a oil well, gushing in all of this money, right, boys? And to think. It's all legit. Not like that other shit we used to do. Beatin' up people and breaking their legs."

Moog started bawling then. He slumped to one knee. He

crawled on the floor toward Big Mike. The men started reaching for their toys.

When he got to where Big Mike was seated, he bent over and started cleaning Big Mike's shoes with his tongue. Big Mike kicked him in the teeth, knocking out a couple. He lay there for a moment, sobbing. Finally, Mike said: "OK, boys. Get him outta here."

When Moog awoke he was lying in a trash can next to the Acme Record skyscraper. Blood was all over his clothes. One of the many thieves who were crawling the urban nights was running away with his shoes. He didn't know what to do now. He'd laid out a couple of million for that synthesizer. All he'd have to do would be to program some funk, hip hop, salsa, rap, blues, rock and roll, rock, rockabilly, C&W, bossa nova, heavy metal, African pop, bluegrass, and he usually would have an album in twenty-four hours. Moog headed back to his house.

17

Nance was hanging back, sucking on some scotch which he held in one hand, and, in the other, a shrimp and seaweed hors d'oeuvre. It was one of those U.N. parties, attended by people from all over the world, wearing the costume of their country. Some people were dancing to the native music of Gun, the African country that was hosting the reception. Phillip and Virginia, who'd gotten him into the party, were talking to some of the guests, and Phillip was thrusting his finger into their faces. He hated Phillip. Sometimes, while asleep, he thought of Phillip fucking his wife, his ex-wife, Virginia; he'd have to get out of bed and smoke a cigarette and couldn't get back to sleep. That was before he became celibate. Weary of checking potential sex partners' antibody status, he had sworn off sex. Now he could go through life without worrying about somebody penetrating somebody else, an obsession of his for the first thirty years of his life when being in love was like being the goalie in a game of ice hockey, trying to prevent somebody's net from being pucked. He remembered about three months into his celibacy, the dream that came. These people from outer space were lining up

American women and shoving them onto spaceships. They were the only ones who wanted them, he figured. American men with their mail-order brides were standing on the sidelines cheering, and his Jewish dentist who'd converted to Islam was standing with his new lady, and he was kinda leading the cheers. When one of the creatures pushed Virginia in she looked to him for assistance and he ignored her; he pretended that he didn't know her, and that Flipachino who had threatened him about her daughter was putting up one hell of a fight, and when the spaceship took off, about three hundred feet up, they dropped her from the flying saucer. He awoke smiling. Celibacy meant that he could screw the women all of the time in his dreams. He could imagine what some of those guys up there next to the Pope dreamed about. They must have gotten surprises all of the time, like Robert Mitchum did in the scene where he returned to his motel room, and Jane Russell was lying on his bed. You couldn't see her face for her bosom.

He was enjoying himself, swaying to the music, and admiring the Xmas decorations. Suddenly a commotion broke out in the middle of the room. He arrived at the scene just in time to see a man slap a woman and send her sprawling on the floor. Her dress slid up around her tan thighs, a sight that didn't escape many of the men, regardless of the nationalities; even the American and British diplomats were staring at them. He recognized those thighs at once. They belonged to his friend, the journalist, Jamaica Queens. Noticing that some men were staring, she held her jaw and began to feign a scream. The man, a Latin-looking person, who wore a black eye patch and a prominent scar that stretched from his left eye to his jaw, approached Jamaica again and started to kick her when Nance walked up and knocked the fellow flat on his ass. A number of Latins ran up to assist him, and about fifty seconds later he came to and began to moan, blood trickling from the corner of his mouth. Jamaica was holding on to Nance's arm, looking down at her date. Virginia was standing next to her friend, and she was smiling at Nance. Her friend noticed the smile and glowered at Nance. Somebody mentioned the man's name. Nance had read about him in the newspapers. He was the famous death squad leader and arms merchant. His friends helped him to his feet, and he approached Nance, said some words in Spanish, and left the party. "What did he say?" Nance asked Jamaica Queens. "He's challenged you to a duel," she answered calmly, with a slight smile.

"He what?"

"A duel. He's quite good at it. In his own country he's killed about twelve men. Don't worry, Nance. I'll talk to him again. He's very jealous. He became angry because he saw someone light my cigarette. He treats me so mean. He's such a knave and a crook," she said, gazing at the man and his entourage as they left. Some of his friends looked back at Nance. One of them ran his finger across his throat. As they exited a couple entered the room. Whoever they were, they must have been important, because the cameras began to go into action. People surrounded them. A man who some said was the Ambassador rushed up to the couple, making his way through the press and admirers who were excitedly making comments and asking questions.

Nance and Jamaica Queens joined the others. He liked her arm on his. She knew that he liked it, her hip bumping against his, and he wondered if she did this to excite him or rather whether this was merely her style. It didn't excite him. The night before he had fucked Cleopatra, Queen of the Nile. He found as he listened to the man that this was the

Prime Minister of Gun. The herald of a new Africa. One who would combine the high technology of Korea and Japan with the old traditional ways. One who was at home with the music, art, and literature of many cultures, who could converse as well about Bauhaus as Muslim architecture. Someone who knew about Western democracy as well as the old associations and clans.

The West was on the decline because it got stuck in a single design, modernism, and its intellectuals and politicians couldn't grapple with the eclecticism of the twenty-first century. Africa, the continent which most had left for dead after the famines and plagues of the 80s, was making exciting gazelle-like leaps into the late 90s, and South America and the Caribbean were hitting their stride. They were calling this Prime Minister, who was so simple and elegant that he came to the party in economy class, the gust of transformation that was taking place on the continent. He called his own movement toward African renaissance Nostromham. Nance came up in the 60s and didn't want to hear about his plans and his missions. He'd seen too many visionaries lying on the balconies of motels and the kitchen floors of hotels, their lives oozing out in rentable ballrooms or in the backseat of a car.

"I'll buy you a drink, Jamaica."

"Thanks for the offer, Nance, but I think I'll take a rain check. I'm living in Soho now." She handed him a card. "Stop by some time. I have to tell you a strange story I heard while I was down in Dominica on assignment." A yellow cab finally pulled up. She got in. She looked at him for a moment. A few years before he would have asked her for sex. He shook her hand instead. Besides, who knew what was in store for him this night. Maybe Irene. The one that Leadbelly said he would get in his dreams. He started home, whistling.

18

"I was the first in my family to try smoking, the first to play hooky from school, the first to venture away from home, and the first to go to jail. On the other hand, I was the first child in the family to own a Cadillac, the first to have a formal wedding, the first to fly to Europe, the first to earn a half million dollars, and the last one to admit that I was wrong."

The Pope was inside his Vatican apartment, reading Chuck Berry's autobiography and shaking his head in disgust, when Cardinal Malidori walked in. He was black haired and wore a black goatee. The Pope shoved the autobiography into a desk drawer. His face was as that of a Cameroon antelope mask. Malidori had eyes like a sparrow. He bowed, and the Pope noted a touch of sarcasm in his voice when he said "Your Holiness." *These dagos still haven't gotten used to a foreign Pope. They'd prefer one of their own. Have to be careful or they'll bump me off the way they did Pius and John, and I wouldn't be surprised if they had a hand in hitting John Paul. I'll bet they hired that mad Turk. They just can't stand a non-Italian in my place. Just like Mussolini said about the Italians. A nation of waiters,* the Pope thought.

"Yes, what is it, Malidori?"

"Your suspicions were correct, Your Holiness." *Your Holiness. That's a laugh. The Romans were the center of the world when his ancestors were crawling around central Asia on their hands and knees, eating goat's cheese. What was the joke our friends, the Nazis, used to make about them? Why the Slavs. Nobody knows where they came from. Ha.*

"We put all of the material into the Vatican computer. Contraceptives, bio–birth technology, birth control, homosexual priests, divorce, married priesthood, women priests, and all of these other demands. It sounds like Old Nick out to embarrass us again."

"I knew it. Who else would it be," the Pope said, rising from his breakfast. "Why in the old days women used to cling to his effigy in order to become pregnant, and he tolerated all manner of loose immoral behavior. He advocated a married priesthood back there in the Middle Ages, and his position toward the devil has always been weak. This Black Peter character, for example. One version has it that this creature was originally exorcised from somebody's body, but instead of destroying this fiend, Nick hired him. So he's the one who is raising such a fuss among the American church, and up to now we thought it was merely some of those Irish priests, Druids in priests' clothing. But now he's back. The rascal is as irrepressible as voodoo. In fact, what is the custom of leaving cakes and delicious things before chimneys for him but idolatry? The Calvinist Walich Sieuwerts knew. Filling shoes with all sorts of sweets. Nothing but sacrifice to an idol. Voodoo plain and simple."

"There have been new developments. Black Peter is also back. And if Nick sees that he'll surely want to engage the creature in a contest. Word has it that Nick is losing his touch."

"But I thought Black Peter was an impostor."

"Yes, there is an impostor. Remember we sent someone to investigate from the Office of the Holy See, and he turned up missing, but before he disappeared he informed us that Black Peter was an impostor."

"But if Black Peter is an impostor, why doesn't Nick contest him? Why would he waste his time?"

"Because the real Black Peter is back in action. He's going about the United States performing intimate miracles. He arrived there to deal with the other Black Peter, but he usually becomes diverted from his true goals; he just can't resist helping those in distress."

"So Nick is probably going to show up on the scene too?"

"You know what a ham he is. How he likes to make appearances."

"This couldn't happen at a worse time. We're in a great contest with the Antichrist, a great eternal adversary, and we're losing the battle."

"There's also a little matter about cash, Your Excellency. Our debtors say they can't wait any longer and they're going to attach a lien to some of our property."

"Can't they understand, Malidori, that we're locked in a struggle that goes on twenty-four hours per day, that he is using subterfuge to undermine our belief in absolutes, that relativism, deconstructionism, positivism, and other philosophies are winning over intellectuals of the West? They don't realize that Satan is real! That Satan is behind deconstructionism, genetic engineering, liberation theology, and pro-choice. The devil is behind this move to bring us down!"

"Yes, Your Holiness, I understand that, but the creditors

are simple, crude men. They're threatening to turn Saint Peter's into a hotel. They want to turn Vatican City into a complex of motels, shopping malls, and upscale boutiques. Surely Satan can wait—"

The Pope's blue eyes cut Malidori like a laser, and his hair seemed to be in flames. Malidori withered under the Pope's presence. The Pope was feeling pretty good up to that moment. In fact, he'd felt good all day, whistling over his breakfast, even eliciting stares from the other cardinals. The night before, he dreamed that he'd returned to his apartment after a full day, and the Virgin was sitting on his bed. All she was wearing was a head covering, and she took that off too. After she removed it she shook her hair, and the hair fell across her back. He woke up and the sheets were bloody. He didn't tell anybody. "I'm sorry, Your Excellency, I misspoke."

The Pope went to the window and stared out over the plaza. Pigeons were walking about the fountain, and there were tourists looking up at his balcony, or taking pictures.

"Malidori."

"Yes, Your Excellency?"

"How do you, well, the devil, how do you suppose he looks?"

Malidori paused. He stroked his goatee. "I imagine him to look like Billy Dee Williams, the American actor, an absolutely fascinating and devastating charmer."

"Malidori, I want to be alone." Malidori exited, bowing and crossing himself. If they knew about his dream, the Italians and the Spanish would read him out of the Church. It was along about three in the morning. He was restless. He was about to go to the chapel when the infernal one stood before him. He was built like a wrestler, and wore black leotards and black boots. He had the head of a goat. And what he did to him made him feel so delicious that he was wondering about his sanity. Again, the devil offered him the contract, but Malidori had enough self-control not to sign.

But he was getting weak. How long would he be able to hold out?

19

Fryer Moog awoke, or rather came to. He heard a quiet snare. He looked up and on the other side of the room, sitting at the drums, accompanying a short man wearing dark glasses and playing the trumpet like an angel, was the man who, in admiration, many musicians called Klook-a-Mop.

"Hey, dudes, what's happening," Moog said, or something maybe even cornier, "Klook-a-Mop, my man," he continued. He tried to rise and approach the dark corners of the room where the two men were playing what sounded like "A Night in Tunisia," but Moog fell over on his back. Klook-a-Mop glanced up at the other man whose black velvet wings stuck out from beneath his armpits. He was going over some passages with a muted trumpet.

"You always was a corny Negro," Klook said. Klook was also short and dark. He looked more like a church deacon than a jazz musician. He was wearing a rich Parisian silk scarf, navy blue double-breasted jacket and grey slacks. He was dressed like Jelly Roll Morton, in the famous photo where Jelly holds a baton as though it were a magic wand. "Look at that shit all over you, and that music these people in

Hollywood got you writing sound like audio heroin or something." The trumpeter wandered off into the darkness of the
room, and played to himself, softly. "I remember you when
you came into Dizzy's band. You were seventeen then. You
were writing these strange but fresh arrangements, and you
played some good trombone, too. You lived in that dingy
walk-up on the Lower East Side. You must have been about
140 pounds."

"But I had to grow, Klook. I'm doing better than that. I'm
rich and famous. They play my stuff all on the radio. I get
a Grammy every year. I have a house that's like the castle at
Disneyland. I'm driving three Rolls Royces. One of them
has gold wiring in it."

"Yeah, but where are you in the music? Where's Moog?
If it weren't for that synthesizer where would you be? Shit
sounds tingly like the stuff they play in amusement parks.
The music has as much sound as a toy xylophone, and has
no personality, no individuality. And that boy. Man, you've
ruined him. Sucker go around wearing an S and M mask
with a zippered mouth, and spent five million dollars jetting
his entourage to Australia so's he could find a pygmy dino-
saur. He wants to prove that the birds descended from the
dinosaurs." The musician in the shadows burst out laughing.
"Ain't nothing but a freak. I smell you all the way over here,
you stink so. That free basing has brought you lower than a
fucking sewer rat. Where's your dignity?"

"You're jealous, that's all," Moog answered, his speech
slurred. "You went to Europe because you couldn't make it
here. I know all about you. You're like the rest of them. Mad
about my success. Those pictures I've made and—"

"Yeah. Those pictures. You and these black people down
here in Hollywood do anything for cash, huh?" Klook shook

his head. "No use trying to persuade you. Man, I feel sorry for you. All that talent. A musical cripple, relying on machines. I'll bet you haven't picked up your horn in years."

"But this is the new thing. I mean, this is what's happening. I don't need no musicians. It saves money. Don't you understand, money." But nobody was there to listen. Klook and his trumpet-playing friend disappeared. And in his place stood Black Peter.

"Listen to him, Moog. He was trying to tell you something."

"Who are you," Fryer Moog said. Black Peter stood in the corner. "How did you get in here. I locked every door. So, you another nigger trying to give me advice. I don't need no advice. I don't need none of you niggers. I got Grammies and Emmies. I made one million dollars last year—"

"Yeah, and it all went to you and the free basing activities of your friends. Your brain has abandoned you. All it does now is turn tricks for hubba. You've given up your life and your career for a few hits of the pipe."

Moog began to sob.

"If you took a CAT scan right now you'd discover all of the little strokes you've had. Do you know why you gave your computer away and forgot it, forgot about your bills—it's because you don't remember things with that bile in your brain." Black Peter flashed an image to the wall. It was Fryer Moog in one of the great 50s big bands, blowing a trombone solo that wouldn't quit, as rich as Frank Rossolino's, as sensual, humorous, and funky as Bennie Green's, and as technically dexterous as J.J. Johnson's, with Jimmy Cleveland's speed and Kai Winding's melancholy and irony.

"You remember all of the promise you had before you

came to Hollywood? Man, jazz needs good composers, and you were one."

Black Peter threw another image upon the screen. A scene inside one of those cheap funeral homes. The scene was holographic and Peter and Fryer Moog entered. They walked down the aisle and looked into the coffin. It was Fryer Moog. An old woman was the lone mourner. Her face was covered with a veil. She lifted the veil. It was his mother. Moog woke up screaming.

20

The New York literary crowd had turned out at the Algonquin to Cedric Longsfellow's farewell party (that wasn't his real name). But though he was the guest of honor, he stood in the middle of the room, ignored. Everybody surrounded Bee-chiko Mizuni, author of a new book that all of the critics were raving about: *Intervention or Internment*. The book, dedicated to all of the G.I.'s who guarded the Japanese Americans at Tule Lake, proposed that the American army had rescued Japanese-American women from the misogyny of Japanese-American men by placing them in the internment camps. She said that Japanese-American men who wrote fiction and nonfiction complaining about the internment experience were perfectly willing to indict the racism of the white soldiers but were not willing to face their own evil, their misogyny. She got her face on the cover of a big mag-azine, *Sister*. She was on the talk shows, and there was a big fight between Okra Hippo and Virginia over who would have her on which show. Okra won out, because her show had the biggest budget, and also, it could be added, the biggest tits, a fact that wasn't lost on Mr. Whyte, producer of "Whyte

B.C." It was said that on an especially windy New York day, she had to be held down for fear that she might float off somewhere, her tits were so big. Beechiko said that the internment provided her with the best years of her life; her Japanese male critics' criticisms were traced to jealousy. They were accused of temper tantrum throwing. James Globe, the new editor of *Organic Society*, a magazine that Cedric Longsfellow had founded in the 1940s, had been brought in to manage the magazine by its new owners, the Slutts, a Midwest family that had made its fortune in mattresses. They too wanted to make Chicago the Athens of America. Globe was a member of the National Critics Society and had already nominated Beechiko Mizuni for a Book Award. He was dressed all in black leather and his Harley Davidson was parked outside. Nobody noticed Longsfellow when he went to the cloakroom. He was about to leave when Beechiko approached him, after breaking through the circle of her well-wishers.

"Mr. Longsfellow, please wait."

"O, Beechiko," he said, putting his arm about her tiny waist.

"Mr. Longsfellow, I apologize for the way you were treated."

"The crude way they fired me, don't worry, Beechiko, it's just the sign of the times. Everything, values, culture, are oozing back into the primeval slime. People hate excellence. Well-rounded characters. Characters that you can feel for, sympathize with."

"You know how much I agree with you, Mr. Longsfellow. I, too, like characters who come alive on paper. Books with a beginning, middle, and an end. I learned all of this working under you. These people who've bought you out. The Slutts. They have no class, no culture. I loved that farewell piece of yours, Mr. Longsfellow. About there being no characters in contemporary literature that one could respect. I agree wholeheartedly with that, Mr. Longsfellow." Mr. Longsfellow had been her mentor. She trusted him more than she trusted her father, a backward San Francisco realtor, who prayed to the false superstitious idols of Buddhism. She was mad at the Japanese for not producing a Tolstoy. A Rembrandt.

"Well, I must be going, Ms. Mizuni." The people in the background were partying back. Once in a while James Globe would glance at Longsfellow, sneeringly. Longsfellow hated Globe, who'd made a career as a neoconservative hatchet man, bashing black and women's studies. Why, the man actually believed that there were intellectuals in Chicago! Must be some move on his part to get a grant, Longsfellow thought. Today's generation was so market oriented. Cared little about aesthetics. He was attending parties with Sartre and Simone de Beauvoir when James Globe was in grammar school. Mr. Longsfellow headed out of the Algonquin and into the snowy New York streets. A young blonde, sables around her ankles, was holding up her date, a man dressed in a smart camel's hair overcoat and white scarf; he was wearing a tuxedo and black shoes, and was trying to blow on a party horn. Down the block Longsfellow could see a homeless person wrapped up in bundles, crouched in the doorway of a dilapidated hotel.

"Mr. Longsfellow, please wait." Beechiko had followed him out of the hotel.

"Yes, Ms. Mizuni." For Mr. Longsfellow it was an effort to get the words out. He preferred Mrs. and Miss.

"I . . . didn't want to tell you this, but I've quit *Organic Society* magazine. I just don't want to stay on without your editorial guidance. I just received a one hundred thousand dollar advance to do a book on Japanese-American male chauvinism. You know, their Samurai Complex. I won't be working on it all of the time, and so I was wondering, since your wife died and all, maybe—maybe I could work for you?"

"But I couldn't afford—I mean, the Slutts may be unscrupulous dilettantes but they gave me a price for the magazine that should enable me to continue living the kind of life I'm accustomed to. I don't think I can afford your services."

"I'll do it for free," Beechiko said. "For you, Mr. Longsfellow, I'll do it for free."

Mr. Longsfellow was so touched that he almost cried. He embraced Beechiko, laying his head on her shoulder. She ran her fingers across the back of his neck. Under a lamppost near the end of the corner, a group of carolers began to assemble. The Salvation Army trumpet started up: "Joy to the World."

21

It didn't take long for Beechiko to establish herself in Longsfellow's Greenwich Village four-story brownstone. She supervised the housecleaning, which was done by Samantha
and Teddy Crawford, a black couple from Saint Albans. She
nearly drove them crazy. Pointing out dust under the bed,
and on the living room furniture they'd missed. Demanding
that they clean the stove every week. Insisting that they do
windows. Sometimes she would entertain Mr. Longsfellow's
guests after they'd had their brandy and conversation, usually
dealing with the lowering of cultural standards in the United
States, or as one of their intellectual heroes said, the descent
into the primeval slime. She would sing ancient songs accompanying herself on the koto, and for very special occasions she would entertain Mr. Longsfellow's gentlemen friends
with Shirabyoshi dances which dated to the reign of the
Emperor Toba (1107–1123). The men would applaud po-
litely and Beechiko would serve the white men tea. She was
happy serving Mr. Longsfellow and writing, in the evening,
her second book about the treatment of Japanese women in
the novels of Japanese men. Having indicted most of the

Japanese male writers in history, she was completing her last chapter on sexism. Her first book was receiving good reviews. The publisher had hailed it as a New Year's Eve for Japanese-American women, and the Japanese men who criticized the book were dismissed as mysogynists.

Mr. Longsfellow enjoyed her too. They spent until the early mornings discussing John Updike's theology, and V.S. Naipaul's trenchant comments about the Third World. She was having the time of her life except for two things. Her appearance. She'd tried to do something about her eyes, you know, well, to make them more modern. She hated what for her was an ugly Japanese face. But that didn't bother her as much as the fact that she wasn't a blonde. Another famous editor she'd had a crush on had already run away with a big old blonde. Mr. Longsfellow had married a blonde shiksa too. His first wife gazed down at her from an oil portrait that hung on the wall above the staircase. She hated her features. Sometimes she'd cry herself to sleep, wishing that she was a blonde. Her second problem was the Crawfords. They were insolent. Always muttering under their breaths.

One day they had it out. It was late morning, and Mr. Longsfellow had been up all night with some friends, discussing Great Books, and the Crawfords were preparing breakfast. Beechiko was already upset. She had an early morning conference with her editor, and had returned to the Village on the subway. There was a handsome couple sitting across from her. The man looked like Martin Sheen; the woman resembled Christie Brinkley; the child was the most beautiful kid you'd ever want to see, and she started playing with the child. The couple wouldn't give her the time of day. Wouldn't even look in her direction. She had been so hurt.

"I told you that Mr. Longsfellow wouldn't be eating that sort of breakfast anymore."

"Don't tell me, Beechiko, or whatever your name is. Mr. Longsfellow has been drinking coffee for thirty years. He loves bacon and eggs. Everything was fine till you come here, you old two-dollar whore," Samantha said, slamming the utensils on the table.

"You ain't doing nothing but gettin' in the way. I have a good mind to take my fist and jam it in your jaw," her husband threatened.

"That's it. Resort to violence. I've read a lot of books about your type. Besides, I'm looking after Mr. Longsfellow's welfare. He is a man who, as you know, has very high standards. You call this breakfast?" She picked up the bacon and held it close to her face. "Look at this grease." She turned up her nose.

Beechiko took the plate and started to dump the eggs, hash browns, ham, and bacon into the trash can. Crawford grabbed her while Samantha took over the plate. Beechiko flipped Crawford's 230 pounds over her shoulder and then, using the bacon, began a pulling contest with Samantha. That's how Longsfellow found them, yelling and screaming at the top of their lungs. He was dressed in a kimono that she'd bought for him. He wore fur-lined slippers whose exquisite leather bore a brilliant sheen. How handsome he looks, Beechiko thought.

"Here, here what's the matter?" Mr. Longsfellow said, looking from one to the other.

"She come in here giving orders. Samantha and I have been serving you for thirty years now, Mr. Longsfellow. We served your wife. I sho do miss her," Crawford said. Mr. Longsfellow lowered his head.

"Me too," Samantha said. "Sweet as she could be. Long blonde hair," Samantha said, looking toward Beechiko with an evil grin.

"She whatun nothin' like this old yellow bitch. Who ever named her Beechiko named her right, cause she ain't nothin' but a bitch, old skinny evil thing."

"That's not called for, Samantha. Crawford. We'll be civil in my house, and I don't want to ever hear you call Beechiko that name again, do you hear?" Beechiko folded her arms and smiled.

"Yes, Mr. Longsfellow," the Crawfords said, unanimously.

"Now my bedroom needs straightening up. Get to it."

"Yes, Mr. Longsfellow." The Crawfords exited, glancing over their shoulders at Beechiko, who was enjoying herself. Longsfellow lowered his white-haired head again and hobbled toward the breakfast table. He sat down, and Beechiko began serving him tea.

"I'm just looking out for your welfare, Mr. Longsfellow. The bacon is full of sodium nitrite."

"Thanks for all you've done for me, Beechiko; what is this?" he said, staring at a bowl that Beechiko placed before him containing miso soup.

"This is your new breakfast, Mr. Longsfellow."

"What would I do without you," Mr. Longsfellow said. He held her hand for a long while. She winked to herself.

With Mr. Longsfellow's vote of confidence, Beechiko ruled the roost. She made the Crawfords' lives miserable, being constantly on their case, prying into their cleaning schedule, going after them for every particle of dust they overlooked, for every faint ring in the bathtub. She personally supervised Mr. Longsfellow's meals, and the laundering of his clothes.

Soon, however, her glory would end. Mr. Longsfellow had warned her not to enter the room that had been shut ever since his wife's death. She couldn't resist, and in the course of prying through his wife's belongings came upon her blonde chemotherapy wigs. She was sitting in front of a mirror trying one on when she saw the reflection of her adversary. Samantha was standing in the doorway, leaning against one of its sides, her arms folded and that wicked glint in her eye.

"UUUUUUU. Immon tell. Immon tell, Mr. Longsfellow, he gave orders to everybody not to enter this room, and here you is in here trying on Mrs. Longsfellow's blonde wig. Only me and Mrs. Longsfellow knew about those wigs. You robbing the secrets from Mrs. Longsfellow's grave." Before Beechiko could say anything, Samantha snapped a photo with her Polaroid.

Samantha turned and headed toward Mr. Longsfellow's study where he had fallen asleep on top of some Great Book. He'd left the television set on. Beechiko started after her.

"Please, please don't tell. I'll do anything. Please don't."

"You'll do anything?" Samantha asked.

"Anything, I don't want Mr. Longsfellow to know."

Samantha let go with a grin. She pointed to a closet at the end of the hall. "Go get that vacuum cleaner and follow me."

The Crawfords supervised her now. They made her do all of their chores, and sometimes they wouldn't even come to work and she'd have to cover for them. It got so that they'd show up only for meals that she had to serve them, in between going to the matinees or the track. One weekend while Mr. Longsfellow attended a conference upstate about the wasteland of American culture, they invited all of their friends over, and made her do all of the cooking, and when they finished eating they made her entertain them on the koto, and ridiculed and laughed at her.

She'd bought the mystical hokiness promoted by black feminist writers which held that black women were sort of like Christ figures who were abused by black men, Herods, Satans, and even the best among them, Pontius Pilates, but in the humiliating scene that she'd just endured, the women laughed louder than the men, and had no sense of the sisterhood that bonded her with them. They were different from the black women she met in publishing circles and at literary parties. Elegant matrons. They were drinking up all of Mr. Longsfellow's scotch, and they said motherfucker more than the men. She was in bed now, and she could hear the refrains from the tune "Honkey Tonk," made popular by Bill Doggett. She hated its bass line. Da doom Da doom Da doom Da doom Da. The low-down chicken-pecking vulgar solo made her feel strange in her viscera. She felt a presence in the room. Yes. There before her stood a small figure. The figure began to glow. She recognized him from the newspapers. His face was appearing in all of the Xmas ads. Black Peter. (Black Peter had transformed himself into the image of the post-yuppie Black Peter that the toy makers had designed.)

"I could feel your distress, far away," he said.

"What, I," she wanted to scream, but she couldn't.

"I'm going to grant you the wish that you desire."

"But."

"It may relieve your torment, or it may bring additional problems," he said. Before she could say anything, he disappeared.

22

Tommy awoke, springing up on his pillow. He'd had the same dream. That President Jesse Hatch was wringing his father's neck and his father was protesting by flapping about and jumping up and down on one leg. "What's the matter, Tommy," his aunt said, coming into his room and turning on the lights. She sat down on his bed and embraced him. He cried on her peacock's breast.

"It was that dream again, Auntie. The President, Jesse Hatch, was wringing my father's neck, and then, then a man, he all covered with blood, and my father was hopping about and his neck was gone, and blood was spurting out of his— O Auntie, it was awful."

"You don't have to talk about it," his aunt said. She was peering over her glasses. "Your father's death was very cruel." First his mother and then his father, and now he was living with his aunt who was a widow. Her husband was killed because he was too busy preening. Tommy got up and had some seeds for breakfast. He cleaned himself and prepared to go to school. The breakfast made him feel better, and he waved to his aunt as he gathered his notebooks, crayons, pencils, and backpack.

School was not a pleasant experience for him. The other kids always razzed him. They made fun of his looks, especially. They felt that they were the best-looking creatures in the world. They were always strutting about, preening, and craning their necks. They wouldn't talk to him nor would they play with him and at lunchtime nobody would eat with him. His teacher led the young peacocks in ridiculing turkeys, after which the peacocks would turn to him and laugh or tease him with gobbling sounds. All they taught in school was about peacocks, and how they were the handsomest birds on earth. That their proto-ancestor was a cross between a phoenix and a nightingale and that their shit was like angel food. Turkeys and peacocks were cousins but you wouldn't know it from the way they treated him. It figures, though, if you think about it. Bears and dogs are cousins, too, but whenever you see a photo of them together the dogs are barking at the bears. Tommy Turkey wasn't doing well in school. Not only was he grieving about his father's death, the President and his family having had the tough old bird for dinner, but he was tired of hearing about peacocks. Reading books about ancient dead peacocks. Peacocks were beginning to think of themselves as too gorgeous for the supermarket freezer, in a time when California nurseries were cultivating flowers for adventurous tastes. Marigolds were being served with dinner in Japan. Peacocks could be next.

If it weren't for his aunt reassuring him and giving him confidence, Tommy would have run away to the wild turkeys in the woods. The peacocks wouldn't wander anywhere near them. One day the peacocks were strutting about as usual, being real pleased with themselves, their teacher telling them how great they were, when Black Peter entered. The peacocks cheered because they had seen Black Peter in all of the promotional ads for the department store. They thought that he was the impostor Peter. Some of them had bought Black Peter dolls. The teacher said something about his objecting to this intrusion, and Black Peter turned him into a plate of roasted peacock, commenced to sit down, tie a napkin to his neck, and dig in. Some of the peacocks threw up. Others fainted. One of them tried to run out of the classroom when Black Peter headed him off, and plucked out some of the peacock's feathers. The peacocks were scared. They started making those sounds of peacocks when they get scared. Black Peter stood at the front of the class, slapping his hand with his rod. "Tommy Turkey, would you come to the front of the class?" Tommy Turkey pointed to himself, he was so surprised.

"Yes, you, Tommy." Tommy walked to the front of the room.

"I don't blame you for what you've done to Tommy Turkey, kids, it's your teacher's fault, and the educational system's fault. You just don't know what it means to be a turkey, how turkeys have provided a food supply for the poor over and over again, but I'm sure, Tommy, that you'd prefer that for the Thanksgiving meal soybeans be substituted for turkey." Tommy smiled. Some of the other peacocks smiled. Black Peter opened a large book that he'd brought. The painting was by the black illustrator John James Audubon. It was a picture of a turkey. Not only was it beautiful, but Audubon had commented that the turkey was indigenous to North America. The peacocks had never seen a turkey who looked this beautiful, not in a gaudy way as they did, but understated and quiet. Turkeys subtly changed their colors to express their emotions, another fact that the peacocks had never learned.

"Also, did you know that Benjamin Franklin proposed that the turkey be made the symbol of this country? That *Meleagris gallopavo* is the Latin name for turkeys," the peacocks looked at each other, impressed, "and that turkeys have been given names in many other languages as well, including *pavo*, the name given to turkeys by Christopher Columbus's crew, and did you know that they were called *guanajo* by the Carib Indians, and *guajolote* by the Aztecs, and *chumpe* by the Mayans? Did you know that turkeys have great fight-back, and have survived regardless of their decimation by hunters, and with all of the nobility that the turkey is associated with you give Tommy here such a hard time." The peacocks lowered their heads. "Ridiculing him and calling him derisive names just because some ignorant people have begun to identify the name turkey with Broadway flops and bad crafts-manship. And most of all, though your teacher never told you this," the class looked over at their teacher, all of which was left were some bones on a plate. "Turkeys and peacocks are cousins. It's possible that you have a common ancestor. Finally, before you ridicule Tommy Turkey, think of this. If they weren't eating turkeys for Thanksgiving, they might start to eat peacocks. Don't ever think that you are too pretty for the freezer." The classroom was silent. Black Peter left the classroom. After a while the peacocks approached Tommy Turkey and offered him some of their corn and grain. Tommy smiled and from that day on Tommy never had any trouble at the school of peacocks.

23

Samantha came into her room the next morning. She held
an ice pack to her head, and her eyes were bloodshot. She'd
come to demand that Beechiko clean up the mess that her
guests had made. Mr. Longsfellow would be arriving from
upstate later in the morning. But Samantha took one look
at her and grimaced, "I tole you not to be wearing any more
of Mrs. Longsfellow's belongings." She went to the bed where
Beechiko lay sleeping. All she saw was a heap of blonde hair
sticking out from underneath the covers. She yanked at the
hair and the sleeping person turned toward Samantha. Samantha sobered up real quick, and her hair stood straight
up. "Samantha, who the hell do you think you're talking to?
Have you lost your mind? Go brush your teeth. Your breath
reeks of whiskey," the person said in a husky and hoarse
voice. But Samantha didn't hear all of the reply. She almost
ran through the door, trying to get out of the bedroom.
Beechiko tried to call out to her, but all she heard was a lot
of commotion downstairs, followed by the slamming of a
door. When she got downstairs, the Crawfords' car was turn-

ing out of the driveway. She looked at them out of the window, and when Crawford saw her, his eyes bulged as though he were being strangled. He took another look. He rubbed his eyes. He took off toward Eighth Avenue doing about sixty. Beechiko turned to the mirror that stood in the living room. Her heart almost stopped. She threw her hand up to her face in horror. Just then she heard the key in the door. She tried to run upstairs. She tried to scream. Her thoughts couldn't come together. Her body wouldn't do what her brain wanted. She could not control what she said. She was imprisoned in another's body. Mr. Longsfellow didn't see her at first. He was shocked by the scene in his living room. Liquor bottles all over the place. Dirty plates with half-eaten food on the dining room tables. Cigarette butts and roaches everywhere. The downstairs toilet was stopped up. Longsfellow removed his overcoat and put down his copy of *Salmagundi* magazine. He brushed off the snow and hung his overcoat in the closet. "Crawford, Samantha, and Beechiko, what is the meaning of this?" he shouted upstairs.

And then he saw her. He just stood there for a minute, his eyes not blinking. Beechiko tried to say something, but somebody else's voice came out.

"Wadsworth."

"Grace. My God. Grace. What—" and then Longsfellow thought. For Wadsworth Longsfellow, there was always a rational explanation for everything. He had read that grieving spouses sometimes, after losing a loved one, had a supernatural experience in which they actually saw their dead husband or wife.

"Wadsworth, aren't you glad to see me?"

He thought for a moment. "Frankly, no. Things around

here couldn't be better. For the first time in my life, I'm happy. I've met someone who not only knows how to treat a man, but shares my interests."

"Wadsworth. What are you saying? All of the years we spent together, I thought you were happy," Beechiko found herself saying.

"You never bothered to ask. You were always complaining. Always whining, and I won't forget that last vacation we had together. As soon as we got off the plane in San Juan, you started to complain about the weather, about the hotel, about the room service, and you called the bellhop a dirty Mexican."

"Wadsworth, you little schlemiel, don't you talk that way—"

"I'll talk any way I want, and . . . and here's something that you can roll over in the grave about. I'm going to ask Beechiko for her hand. She's Japanese. She also likes characters who come alive and breathe. She despises postmodernism. One-dimensional trash." Beechiko wanted to run into his arms, but she couldn't, she was paralyzed.

"But, but, she's not blonde," his dead wife said.

"I don't care about that."

"Ha. You who used to burn candles for Marilyn Monroe. You had to go into therapy over that."

"That was the fifties. These are the nineties."

"But what about her . . . her . . . eyes?"—and when she said that pulled back the corners of her eyes. "Stop it. Stop," Mr. Longsfellow said, and she found the body in which she was imprisoned laughing. She wanted to shake the body. She wanted to—and then she awoke. It was quiet downstairs. She dressed and went down. Mr. Longsfellow was seated at his desk. The downstairs was in a mess from where the Crawfords had left it. He rose and walked over to her.

"Where are Crawford and Samantha?" she asked.

"I got rid of them."

"You what?"

"I came back early and they were playing some terrible music. Some bum who had passed out said it was called 'Nighttrain.' It just had this insufferable saxophone solo. It sounded like a tomcat in heat. It assaulted my sensibilities. I fired them, of course; I gave them severance pay." He showed her the photo of her with his wife's wig on. She was embarrassed.

"You don't have to be a blonde, Beechiko. I love you the way you are. I like your hair. I like the texture of your skin. Your eyes . . . so inscrutable." Beechiko smiled shyly. Mr. Longsfellow embraced her for a long time. She looked out of the window, and there winking at her was Black Peter. They winked at each other. He had given her the best Xmas she ever had.

24

Black Peter, the impostor, awoke. He must have blacked out. His last memory was that of him and his cronies trying to top each other in a liquor-imbibing contest. His friends must have left because he couldn't find his wallet. His eighteen-year-old Minnesota Viking was sleeping next to him. Her blonde hair covered a teddy bear. Her hand clutched a half-eaten Mars bar. The ashtray was full of roaches. He'd have to somehow get out of bed, throw cold water on his face, and prepare for another appearance. He had to do everything that Jack Frost told him. He was about to ring for breakfast when Jack Frost burst into the room. His hands were full of newspapers.

"Pete, why didn't you tell us you were doing this stuff? It's terrific. Look at all the great publicity we're getting."

"Huh," Black Peter said. Jack laid the newspapers out on the table. Black Peter rubbed his eyes and examined the press. His chest got tight. He took a second look, and a third.

"Boy is Elder Marse going to be happy when he sees this. Why you and I are liable to get a bonus." On the society pages of the *New York Exegesis* was the announcement of the wedding of Beechiko Mizuni to Wadsworth Longsfellow, former editor of *Organic Society*. They told the press that they were grateful to Black Peter. On another page there was a photo of peacocks with their arms around a turkey. The caption read: Black Peter brings understanding between Peacocks and Turkeys.

"Good picture of you, Pete," Jack said. On the entertainment page there was an announcement that Fryer Moog was opening at some of the Village nightclubs. He'd gotten back his chops and reassembled his quartet from the old days after spending what he called many wasted years in Hollywood. He had gained back some of his weight and jogged every day. You couldn't keep the guy away from juice bars and vegetarian food. He too thanked Black Peter, and there were others. A woman who needed a liver transplant for her child said that Black Peter showed up and contributed the check. A farmer whose family farm was about to be foreclosed said that Black Peter had arrived in the nick of time to rescue him. "Even though I'm a white man, if he were running for President I'd vote for him," the farmer said. And so the stories went.

"And to think, we all thought you were pissing your life away at Xmas parties all over town, and here you were, flying all over the country, rescuing people. The department stores are mobbed. How did you manage to do it, O, tell me sometime about it, Black Peter—" Before Black Peter could say anything, Jack Frost exited the room.

Black Peter poured himself a glass of strong whiskey. He looked outside the window, and he saw people on crutches, as well as with other disabilities, and Third World women desiring blonde hair, blonde women desiring Afros, black men requesting that Peter bless their superman capes, white men begging Peter to teach them how to say hey dude, hey bro, hey home and to do the moon walk, but Black Peter was faced with some heavy "existentialist" questions as a New York Intellectual would say. If he were he, who was *he*? Or, who was doing him while he was doing *him*? His life was becoming like a riddle popularized by Abbott and Costello.

25

Meanwhile, in his apartment in the Netherlands, a cold metaphysical place, somewhere in the Arctic, where the favorite musician is Rudy Vallee, Nick was preparing for his annual visit for the Xmas season; he was pacing up and down, his hands held tightly behind his back. It was December fifth. He was furious, and earlier that morning had fired two elves who'd been assisting him for so many seasons, the other elves had forgotten when they joined the team. His favorite assistant, Destar D'Nooza, was shining his black boots. Mr. D'Nooza had the sad, drooping eyes of a basset hound, and an outstanding nose. In a former life he had served Lord Mountbatten when Mountbatten was the Viceroy of India, an experience for which he had always been grateful and told stories about it to the other elves, who hated him.

"Boss, you zeem so . . . so nervous. What bother you, boss?"

" 'What bothers me,' he asks," Nick said. "You see these headlines that Black Peter is getting?" "Black Peter Cured My Gallstones" read the headline of the *International Herald Tribune*, a newspaper that Nick read every morning.

"O, boss, why should you worry about dat? It's just a Turd World trick to embarrass you. You still on top, boss. The happiest part of my life is bringing a brilliant gloss to your boots."

"You really think so, Destar?"

"Tink so. I knows so, boss. Why dat Black Peter is impostor anyway. We check it out. He speak English very bad, boss. Very bad. He say, we bees, as in, we bees going. He don't know how to conjugate verbs, boss, like I do. I went to school in London—"

"Yes, yes, you've told me a number of times, Destar. But I think you're wrong, I knew about the impostor four years ago when I . . . when I—"

"Boss, don't worry about dat. Don't you worry. You choose wrong man. Dis Dean Clift have no credibility, and so when you make your appearance, though you change him, nobody believe, boss. Wasn't your fault. You have a better idea this time. It will really alter the course of history. You so great, boss, you so—" Destar began sobbing.

"What's wrong, Destar?" Nick said.

"I just tink, boss. I'm so happy to be of service to you. A . . . bug like me, able to do my part for Western civilization."

"You're a loyal elf, Destar, and if you continue such devotion I'll see to it that you get that English country manor you were never able to obtain during your earthly stay."

"O, tank you, boss, tank you, would you like a little lamb dish with some curry before we prepare for our annual journey?"

Nick nodded.

26

Bob Krantz bunked in Nance Saturday's apartment for the night. He was up all night going to the bathroom and occasionally his trips stirred Nance. Krantz woke up screaming several times. He had a bad night. At breakfast the next morning, Krantz told Nance the whole story. Nance sat there, stunned. Reverend Jones and his pretend friends. The possible murder of Admiral Matthews. And most shocking of all, Operation Two Birds. During the Iran-Contra investigation in the 1980s, it had been revealed that Oliver North was part of a plan to round up all of the black leaders and put them in camps. But those plans sounded mild in comparison to Two Birds, which called for low-yield nuclear attacks on cities with surp populations, poor blacks, Hispanics, Asians, no longer the model minority, and the millions of whites who were as useless, nonvital and up to no good like the rest. Nance was shocked. He knew that a lot of people in power were crazy, but not that crazy. A preacher in the White House talking to ghosts. Operation Two Birds. A computerized superhero robot on loan from Hollywood. The murder of the Secretary of Defense.

"Look, Virginia Saturday is my wife. My ex-wife. You could go on her show. Tell the world about it."

"Who would believe it? Look what they did to Dean Clift after he made those claims. They'd do the same thing to me." Nance thought about it. He stroked his heavy mustache. It was so heavy it must have weighed about two pounds.

"Maybe you have a point."

"Besides, I'm still indebted to Reverend Jones. He saved my life."

"But now he's trying to get rid of you. What kind of loyalty is that?"

"Reverend Jones is the only man in America who can stop our country's sinking into the abyss."

"You talking about niggers?"

"No, why get so sensitive? We're not against blacks. There are blacks who are high in the government. The man who now runs Reverend Jones's evangelical empire, Reverend John the Conqueror, is black. He does all of the preaching while Jones advises Jesse Hatch on how to run the government." Krantz looked at his watch. He walked over to the TV set and turned it on.

"Damn, all you do is watch the news all day."

"Maybe there'll be something about—"

Jesse Hatch was answering questions from reporters.

Q: "Mr. President, are you telling us that Robert Krantz developed this whole scheme, that nobody in the White House knew about it?"

A: "That's right, he was going to explode neutron bombs on Miami, New York, and other cities with large concentrations of surps, and blame it on our ally, Nigeria, and then destroy some nuclear generators in Nigeria." Nance looked at Krantz. "It's not true, he's lying," Krantz said. Krantz and Saturday kept their eyes trained on the set.

Q: "Bob Krantz was brought into the White House by Reverend Clement Jones. Has Reverend Jones been informed of this development?"

A: "Reverend Jones is really disturbed about the news, ladies and gentlemen, and he's shocked that Krantz has usurped the power of the Oval Office."

"That can't be so, Jones was in on the plan from the beginning," Krantz pleaded. The camera switched to Reverend Jones. He seemed to be near tears as he told the reporters how Krantz had been like a son to him, and how he was so disappointed that Krantz had gotten involved in such a nutty scheme. Krantz turned off the television set. He sat in a chair, gazing out the window. Nance went over and placed a hand on his shoulder. There was a knock at the door. Nance answered. It was a man. He and Nance talked for a minute, as Krantz sat in the living room of the two-bedroom apartment. Nance and the man disappeared into a room that Nance referred to as his "office." There was a procession of people into the apartment all morning. Men and women. Women with children and babies. This went on until about twelve noon, when Nance said he had to start making his runs to La Guardia.

27

Nola Payne, Supreme Court Justice, wasn't able to finish her address before the National Association for the Advancement of Feminists. She was heckled and treated rudely by those who had fought to make her the second female Justice on the Supreme Court, having become disillusioned with the first one, among whose first decisions was one holding that President Nixon was above the law. Nola was accused, by the feminists, of voting on the side of the patriarchy ninety-nine percent of the time and having abandoned those who had made her.

A questioner had asked Nola about her statement in an op-ed printed in the *New York Exegesis* that women had been crippled by their former oppression and that now was time for a new feminist responsibility and a mature feminism. That the feminists hadn't proven that they had gone beyond the phase of rage and storm. That their problems weren't being imposed from the outside.

She said that they could no longer blame their problems on sexism, but now had to look to themselves, to their own self-destructive behavioral patterns for an explanation for their failure. That the society had become gender blind. She said that they had to change their culture, give up their clinging to men, their Cinderella fixation, their addiction to dependency so that men would accept them. She said that if men discriminated against them—maybe it was their fault.

A woman got up and called her a middle-class bourgeois bitch. When she said something good about her male colleagues on the court they called her a traitor and started to boo her. Somebody asked her about the court's scheduled review of the 13th, 14th, and 15th amendments, the Emancipation Proclamation, and the Dred Scott Decision. She said that the court just wanted to take another look at them, and when someone quoted Reverend Jones's speech quoting Genesis:9 that slavery was a good thing, and that it solved the unemployment problem, and that he needed some hands around his house to help his wife with her watercolors, she said that Reverend Jones didn't have a racist or sexist bone in his body, and that blacks, gays, Asians, and other surps were not carrying their weight, and that this was the reason for the West's decline. Tumult erupted and Nola Payne had to leave by the back entrance. As her chauffeur drove her home she took more than a few swigs from a flask of bourbon she carried around. By the time she reached home, her blood alcohol content was way above that of the legal limit. He had to help her up the steps of her lavish Georgian home, and her maid had to undress her and help her into her nightgown.

Her face was puffy and red. Her blue-tinted hair was becoming unglued. Her round, soft stomach felt like Beirut, Lebanon. The feminists, her former allies, had especially given her a hard time when she announced her support for the Conversion Bill; she said that those who did not pledge allegiance to Reverend Jones's brand of Christianity should be deported.

Why did women hate her so? Why couldn't they understand that the 90s demanded responsible feminism? One that had serious issues to deal with, one that had gone beyond bra burning, sexual preference, and abortion on demand. She had to show that she could take it like a man. Could support tradition and values. That it wasn't like the old days when they were in the Village. Times were more complicated. And what was wrong with a Christian country? Reverend Jones's ideas were a little bit bizarre, but somebody had to stand up against the excesses of the last thirty years.

The maid peeked into the bedroom where Nola lay stretched out on her big bed. Sometimes the maid would find fifteen or sixteen whiskey bottles underneath her bed, or in the closet.

"Your Honor," the maid said.

"Yes, what is it, Maria?"

"Would you like something before I go, Señora?"

"No, Maria, I think that I'll just get some sleep."

"Those women treated you awful, Madame. I saw it on television. All of that pushing and shoving. It's amazing that you were not hurt, Madame."

"Thanks, Maria." The woman started out the door. "You have plans for this evening?" Nola asked.

"We're having a Xmas party, just members of my family."

"That must be nice."

"Yes, Señora. I must go now. Merry Xmas, Señora."

"Merry Xmas, Maria."

She went to sleep. It began to rain. Shango hammered the sky. She awoke about one a.m. and put her hand on the table. Someone was calling her name. Nooolllaaa. Nooolllaaa. The French doors to the bedroom swung open. She could see the lights of Washington in the distance. She sat up. She went to close the French doors. She hated being all alone in the house. At fifty she was still young, and some men found her attractive when she was sober, but there was no time for dates. She was all work. She drove her law clerks seven days a week, and since she had become Chief Justice, she worked even harder. She was in her bed alright, but it seemed to be suspended. She wasn't alone in the room. "Who's there," she called. She could make out a man in black robes. His back was turned to her. She could make out some of the words he was saying. "Yet fear, still more, the still fearful doom / That takes the richest of heaven's slighted gifts / And leaves thy body and thy soul in darkness / To roam the earth a senseless corpse, or gives thee / Before thy time, to the tormenting fiends / Such was my crime—with life, health, reason blest / And heart with rapture glowing, I looked round / Such was my punishment; the beam from heaven / That pours its light into the mind of man / Was suddenly extinguished, and a shroud / Darker than that of death, enveloped all / Within me and around me. In this gloom / Peopled with specters, filled with scenes terrific / How long I lived—of the dread agony / Could life be called—I know not. To the dead / and the condemned. Time measures not his steps / And every moment seems eternity."

The poor man turned to her. She started to scream but the specter seemed harmless. It was shimmering in a pale green light. She could identify his face, wrinkled, gaunt and crawling with maggots. There was a huge hickey located above his eye. He wore a wig which had become the home for many insects. It was Judge Taney, the man who had been a Supreme Court justice when Dred Scott came before the court, in 1857. The case of Sullivan vs. Scott where a slave sued his master for freedom after the master transported him into a free territory.

"I could have had that beam of light, Nola Payne," Taney said. "I had the education: Greek, Latin, standards, tradition were all mine. I was in the right social class and had all of the breaks, but I met my match when Dred Scott came before me; he had something that I didn't have. A slave as lowly as he was. I had such a contempt for the African. I said that he had no rights that a white man was bound to respect, and when he came into the courtroom, I couldn't take my eyes off him. What dignity.

"O, if only they had had black studies in my time. If only I had become acquainted with Ivan Van Sertima, if only I could have spent some time at the feet of James Spady instead of in those schools where I was taught that the white man was the center of the universe and that women and blacks were put here to be their slaves. Scott had courage, but I made the wrong decision. A decision etched forever in the annals of law, and I am condemned to wander around the American hell discarded by history like the Spruce Goose, my name spoken with disgust. Bewarrreee, Nola Payne. Bee-warreee. This Reverend Jones is a dangerous man, and the Conversion Bill is bad news. Why, if the Jews and blacks are thrown out of the country, it will become dull and phlegmatic, like Canada. And so I'm condemned to wander eternity, reciting my brother-in-law Francis Scott Key's awful poetry. Would you like to hear the choruses that were omitted from 'The Star-Spangled Banner'?"

"That won't be necessary, Chief Justice Taney." Nola turned

to the voice that was standing at the threshold of the garden. There attired in priestly clothes was Nick.

"Who are you?" she asked.

"Nicholas of Bara," Nick said. "Chief Justice Taney is giving you good advice."

"But they all said that Clift was making it up."

"They were wrong."

"It is you, isn't it?" Nola said, now sitting up in her bed.

"It's me. Clift was right. He did the right thing. You do the right thing, or you, too, will become like Taney. A man brought to disgrace by vanity." Nola Payne began to sob. And when she awoke the next morning, the sun was so bright that it burnt through her eyes, and it was only eight a.m. It would be a beautiful Xmas day. She called the justices into special session. She rose and went into the bathroom and removed the pills from their cabinets and watched as they went down the toilet. She went into the library and took all of the whiskey out and poured it down the sink. She took a bath and thought for a long time. She knew what she had to do, after Roger Taney's pitiful narration of his infamous role in the Dred Scott decision. She prepared her own breakfast and ate in the garden. She walked down the stairs and got into her limousine. Her chauffeur was shocked. This was the first time in five years that he didn't have to help her down the stairs, as she was recovering from a drunken stupor. She arranged for a special session of the Court. She went to the Court and cast votes that would shake Jesse Hatch's administration to its foundation. She wrote the majority opinions for the vote against the Conversion Bill and for overruling a lower court by handing the reins of power to Dean Clift, who had been wrongfully removed from office by the Hatch administration.

28

As soon as it was heard that Nola Payne had cast the vote, restoring Clift to the Presidency and striking down the Conversion Bill, anybody who had anything to do with the Hatch administration began making travel arrangements. By late afternoon, the White House was almost empty. Committees in both the House and the Senate began announcing investigations into the Terrible Twos—Operation Two Birds— the covert operation that had been begun in the Clift administration. Everybody was abandoning Reverend Jones and going over to Dean Clift. Jesse Hatch had gotten in touch with officials of the returning Clift administration to arrange for the best possible deal that he could get for his role in the Terrible Twos. He didn't want to do all that much time in Leavenworth. Kingsley Scabb had contacted some of his friends about a lectureship on the role of the Vice President at one of the staid Eastern universities. Nola Payne was being cheered everywhere she went and was being mentioned as a possible candidate for Governor of California, a state that seemed to be created just for her. Reverend Jones was gulping down a lot of pills and drinking water. He turned on the other channel. There was James Way, the hard-boiled conservative columnist, inside his Georgetown home, with homeless people sitting at his table, and welfare children opening their presents underneath his tree. The local TV cameras cornered him in the kitchen, supervising the chefs who were roasting turkeys or roast beef and Yorkshire pudding for all of the surps who were lined up in front of his house. His neighbors had complained, but he paid them no mind. Excerpts from the column that had appeared in the *Washington Sun* earlier that day told the whole story. "I went to hell and back with Nicholas. He showed me Walter Winchell, who was there for insulting Josephine Baker, and Westbrook Peglar for saying nasty things about Eleanor Roosevelt. . . . You get nowhere in this world with a nasty temper, and by using invective. . . . You get nowhere in this world without compassion and mercy," he had written. The live TV cameras were trained on him as he scooped some potatoes and placed them on the plate of a homeless surp. "Thank you," the grateful man said. "I use to not be able to get through a column without citing at least three dead men from the canon, but now I'm thinking for myself. I'm tired of being Joe Bob Briggs with a Thesaurus, and I've decided to modify my wordy style. I've thrown away my Bartlett's. I feel honest. I feel fresh. And I'm going to quit being the mean and petty little son of a bitch whose whole career was built on baiting black people," Way told the interviewers at the conclusion of the meal. The homeless surps began to applaud James Way, the columnist. Tears began to stream down his cheeks like Niagara Falls. One of the homeless approached him and put his arms around him. He cried into the man's chest, reminding one of the photo of Nixon crying into Ike's chest, after his famous Checkers speech.

Reverend Jones was shaking his head in disgust. He turned the channel to C-Span. Some of the meanest Congressmen were taking turns recounting the supernatural experiences they'd had with Nick. Fighting each other over who was going to introduce subsidized housing for the poor, universal health care, free day care, scholarships for all students, etc. Nick was all over.

Everybody had deserted the White House. The doorbell rang. The Marines and the Guards had gone downtown to gawk at Dean Clift and his party, like everybody else. Reverend Jones called for the help. "Jane, Esther, get that door, on the double," he shouted. There was no answer. He'd forgotten that it was Xmas Day. He had to go and answer it himself. He would have to do a lot for himself from now on.

His wife had called him that morning and told him that she was going to spend the holidays with her folks in Wisconsin, and not to expect her back. That Saint Nicholas had come to her in a dream and told her that she had too much talent to waste it on the same scene. That she could return to the University of Wisconsin, at Madison, and develop her gifts. She wanted to be in a place where, as a blonde, she could remain anonymous. She told him that she had dismissed the help, and if he wanted Xmas dinner, he could fix it himself.

Who could it be at the door? He had an hour to catch the plane. By Xmas evening, he'd be in Texas. He'd fight his enemies from his Gospel Hour Show. Call upon his invisible battalions to help defeat the fornicators and whoremongers. He would fight the ungodly from exile in Texas. The knock at the White House door was louder. "OK, I'm coming," Reverend Jones said. "Hold your horses." When he opened the door he got the shock of his life. Standing before him was Lucy Artemis, and rather than the homeless surp she'd become after he'd destroyed her career—baggy, dirty, and disheveled—she wore a cutaway suit and fox skins in wine and lavender. Her lipstick was eye-boggling, and her black eyebrows had been sculpted. Her long grey gloves set off the overall elegance of her appearance.

29

Nance was feeling the Xmas spirit and so he allowed Krantz to hide out in his apartment for a little while longer. He was filling up Nance's small apartment with newspapers and magazines which were in neatly bound stacks in the corner. Nance had decorated the place with Cost Plus rattan, wicker, and cane furniture. Chairs, a sofa, and a coffee table. On the wall hung art by Haitian painters, Jacques-Richard Chery, Wilmino Domond, Prefete Duffaut, Fritzner Lamour, Celestin Faustin's incredible *La Soiree de Damballah*. Its reds, yellows, oranges, and browns warmed the apartment. Out of place among these reproductions was a portrait of Maurice Ravel, the composer. When asked why, Nance said that he admired Ravel as a man who put his testosterone to good use. He'd put on his disguise and go out in the morning for the early papers and then in the afternoon he'd fetch the late editions. His picture was everywhere. Jesse Hatch appeared in a news conference flanked by the head of the F.B.I. and other intelligence officers to announce that all of the borders were being watched in case Krantz had any ideas about leaving the country. He said that he and the members of the administration hadn't the slightest idea that Admiral Matthews and Krantz had been collaborating on an insidious plot to liquidate the surps and promote a war with Nigeria. Hatch said that Nigeria hadn't built nuclear reactors in the first place, and that it had been the hothead prime minister of the newly named country of Gun who was suspected of having plants operating in the desert. Hatch said that the United States had satellite photos of the operation.

Krantz spent a lot of time peeking through the curtains to look out the window. Nance, meanwhile, was making his run for fares to La Guardia. When he wasn't doing that, Krantz noticed that he spent a lot of time in his "office," as he called it. It was in the rear of Nance's small apartment, and contained a desk and two chairs. There always seemed to be a line of people waiting to talk to him. One day Krantz asked him why.

"It's because I'm a 'King.' "

"A what?" Krantz chuckled.

"I'm the king of this block. You'll notice that in the other neighborhoods the streets are filthy, and dealers are openly selling dope; this street is clean and orderly. It could be a street in Bern, or Basel. You don't see any abandoned cars, nor do you see any trash littering the streets. See those flower gardens planted in front of the tenements? That's my idea too."

"I don't understand."

"Of course you don't. You see, you and people like you are always asking why the blacks don't want to move to the suburbs, and why they concentrate in these cities, and why they don't want to climb the ladder. It's because some of them are marooned, by choice from American Society. They don't want to fit in. They don't want to integrate, as the old word used to be, and so these ghettos as you call them are enclaves for the

marooned. They have their own law, and their own leadership, like the Indians. Wherever Africans were carried in the
hemisphere, there have always been the marooned—the run-
away. So on this block I'm the 'King.' I deal with downtown
for them. I put pressure on the crack dealers. I phone in their
license plate numbers to the DMV. I call the Health Department. I take pictures of their transactions. If this block
is the eye of the hurricane, it's because I keep it that way."

"But doesn't that make you a snitch?"

"A snitch. Look, pal, was Harriet Tubman a snitch? She
spied on the Confederate Army, and passed on valuable information to the Union. These crack merchants pose more
of a threat to us than Robert E. Lee did. The way I look at
it, I'm a freedom fighter. If you fuck with this neighborhood,
you have to come by me. We have a neighborhood alert
program here, and look out for the women and the kids."

"Man, you're a real Boy Scout."

"Call it what you want to call it. I see that the old people
on the block get their Social Security checks. I see to it that
the kids don't play hooky from school. I help these people
stave off bill collectors."

"That's irresponsible, Nance."

"I don't know what you're talking about."

"People should be responsible for their debts."

"Why don't you tell that to your boss, Hatch? The U.S. is
rolling up about a million dollars in debt every second, and
you got these defense contractors ripping off the government to
the tune of billions, and you and your friends down in Washington. Nothing but moral rot and hypocrisy. Look at Jesse
Hatch, about to be indicted for a land deal. And that ain't all."

"What's not all?" Krantz asked.

"Every prostitute in New York has his number. They all

know he's a freak. He comes into town about three nights a
week. Some friends of mine who work at La Guardia say
that they hide Air Force 1 over in the shadows of the field,
near a fence."

"Well, if you were a true King you'd instruct these people
to pay their debts."

"They don't have the cash, Krantz. Anyway, all that I'm
doing is perfectly legal. If landlords don't keep their buildings
up to code, I instruct my clients not to pay the rent. And
these bill collectors. You don't know the tactics they use.
These people are behind in their bills, they're likely to be
garnisheed. You just don't know how it is among the surps.
That's your name for them, isn't it? We're surplus. We don't
have the necessities nor are we necessary. But what am I
telling you this for? You're the one who masterminded this
Operation Two Birds."

"Then why are you hiding me?"

"Because I need the cash. Nothing personal."

"You're smart, Nance. You should have finished law school.
You would be a judge or something by now."

"I like doing what I'm doing. A jack of all trades. I live
by my wits." Nance went into the kitchen. He wolfed down
a doughnut. He opened the refrigerator. There were steaks,
fish, chicken, and ground beef in the freezer. There were
also boxes of frozen yogurt and bags of shrimp. The drawer
at the bottom of the refrigerator was filled with fruit and
lettuce. "What's all of this?" Nance asked.

"Just thought I'd pick up a few items. There wasn't anything in the refrigerator but a bottle of Pepsi and a paper plate
full of ribs."

"Look, don't get comfortable. I'll give you until tomorrow
to make other arrangements. After that, I want you out."

*　*　*

Her skin was rich and dark. The color of Embarcadero candy.

"Where's Nance, and who are you?" He couldn't take his eyes off her. She was carrying a baby with her that looked as though it was about three months old. She was wearing a cotton dress. He could tell that she was braless. This fascinated him. She wore her hair in dreds.

"He's out at La Guardia."

"Shit. This man from Con Ed is talking about turning out my lights and he's out at La Guardia. I have a baby who has to have his formula heated and he's out at La Guardia. They're supposed to come this afternoon."

"Why don't you just pay your bills?" She looked at him and made a contemptuous splitch with her lips. She screwed up her nose and looked Krantz up and down. The baby was crying. She turned around and started downstairs. Krantz went to the door.

"Who are you?" she asked, looking him up and down.

"Krantz, Bob Krantz."

"You a friend of Nance's?"

"You might say so. I'm staying with him over the holidays."

The baby looked up at Krantz. It made some infant sounds and balled a fist. She took out one of her breasts and began to feed the child, eyeing Krantz while doing so. She rocked the child. He was impressed with her breasts, which had the elegant curves of modern Italian furniture.

"Do you have a cigarette?" she asked. He got up and went over to a drawer in the kitchen where Nance kept cigarettes. He came back and gave her one. While she leaned over, she bent her head and took a light from him. Their eyes met.

"Nance helps me. I don't have no old man. He went away a few weeks ago to the work-force project. Thought he'd send me some money by now. He's been out of a job for three years." Krantz knew all about the work-force project. Communities located outside of the cities, where unemployed male surps lived in barracks. The conditions were abominable. He was one of their architects. She wouldn't be seeing her husband for a long time. He hated what he did for the Hatch administration, but he had a larger purpose in mind. Something that neither Hatch nor the Reverend Jones knew about. The baby kept crying.

Krantz was taken by her beauty. She had some serious lips and honest eyes. Her craftsman's legs were the color of the dark wood in the Harvard Club. She wasn't like some of the white women he met in Washington, who were as hungry for power as the men, and behaved like them.

"Have you eaten?"

"I had a Hershey bar a couple of hours ago," she said.

"Look, I'll go down to the Chinese take-out place and get some food," he said.

"That would be nice," she said, rocking the child who had fallen asleep. He put his coat on and started out of the door.

"Would you bring me some beer," she said. "I haven't had any beer in a long time." He nodded. They smiled at each other. Outside, the snowstorm was so blinding that he could only see the lights from the street lamps. He turned the corner and almost walked into Joe Beowulf. As Beowulf grabbed him and shoved him into his hubba buggy, a Suzuki Samurai, all he could think of was how cold Beowulf must have been in his Viking clothes, the huge belt, the bear fur covering his crotch, and strapped by leather to his ankles and feet. But then he remembered, as they began their journey toward Washington, that the weather didn't affect Joe.

30

"Lucy! How did you get in here?"

"It was easy. Everybody is downtown, awaiting Dean Clift's return to the Capitol."

"Yeah, that Nola Payne. She deserted me too. All of that junk about Saint Nicholas, and then James Way, and then all of those Congressmen. The whole capital is going nuts. Seeing things."

"So where are you going?"

"I gotta get out of here. All of us will get the slammer. Clift's going to want revenge. Then they'll find out about that dumb Terrible Twos Operation. That Clift was telling the truth when he said that Nicholas told him we were involved in Operation Two Birds. We used that as an excuse to put him away, but now everybody is seeing this Saint. I'd like to get my hands on this Nicholas."

"You'll have your chance."

"What do you mean?"

"He's on the way over here."

"Yeah, well, I'm not surprised that you'd be talking about ghosts. That was your business until I closed you down. You were serving as a medium for Congressmen, cabinet members and their wives."

"I can help you. You see, he can't leave well enough alone. It's not enough that he's influenced the political destiny of the capital, he wants to change you, too. All we have to do is wait."

"But why are you doing all of this?"

"I'll tell you later. Let's get rid of Nicholas first, and then we'll take care of Clift."

"But why are you helping me? I tried to banish you from Washington."

"Saint Nicholas is threatening our operations. Besides, I have a score to settle with him. After we get rid of him, we can go back to our feuding. Besides, I'd like to get my hands on Nancy Reagan's crystal ball. I hear it's hidden somewhere here in the White House."

"But how are you going to get rid of Clift?"

"I have friends in low places," Lucy said.

31

Joe Beowulf was heading toward Washington, his prisoner, Bob Krantz, sitting next to him in handcuffs. He had come to and now was looking out at Pennsylvania farm country. He had a headache.

"Would you like a cigarette," the thing asked. Krantz shook his head.

"Thought you could get away, huh? Nobody gets away from Joe Beowulf. I catches them all. See that? My brain is almost human. You've seen my movies. I catch them all in my movies. I turn over cars. I break down doors."

"I've seen your movies."

"What, you don't like my movies?"

"I didn't say that. They seem to be dependent upon a lot of action shots. Why don't you do the classics? Golem. Frankenstein. There are plenty of roles that a robot can play. High-caliber roles." They rode in silence. Passing through the countryside. Through small villages and towns. Once they were slowed by a horse and buggy driven by an Amish man.

"Wait till I get you back to the Reverend. You did a bad

thing. They said in the newspapers that you did a bad thing. Reverend Jones talks about it all the time. You and that Admiral. He said that you were like a son to him, and that he saved your life, but after he took on the mighty responsibilities of the Presidency you and all of his friends abandoned him. He told Heinrich and me a lot. He said that we were his only friends. He said that if he's around in the next administration he's going to put the Jews and the blacks in adjoining barracks so that they can have bull sessions and debates all night. Ha ha ha. Reverend Jones is a man who thinks ahead. He wants me to stay around until then, and then I can go back to Hollywood, having helped my nation the way Superman and other heroes did."

"You believe that? That you're like Superman? Superman was Azhkenazi. He believed in truth and justice. You believe everything they say. Sure, they may make me take the fall for Operation Two Birds, send me away, have me killed, but they can do the same for you. And what did you get out of your role as Joe Beowulf? You couldn't have received as much as Towers Bradhurst, the producer. He has a home in Santa Fe, Long Island, and a luxury apartment overlooking Central Park. He jokes to his friends that one day he's going to convert you into twist-off caps for the soda company he owns."

"What do you mean?"

"You're last year's model. You can always be upgraded, with a more advanced piece of software. You're nothing but a unit of plastic and aluminum. Why do you think that Bradhurst was so eager to lend you to the government for service? It's because your movies are taking a dive at the box office, that's why. He's thinking about replacing you with a female superhero, Jane Beowulf. It's been on the boards for two years."

"That's a lie."

"Suit yourself." They drove in silence for about five miles until they came upon a gas station. Beowulf slammed on the brakes.

"Where are you going?"

"I'm going to call Towers," he said, twisting his head around to face Bob. "And if you're lying to me, I'm going to break your neck. They won't have to put on a show trial." The creature whose response to every situation was force and violence headed toward the phone booth that was situated inside the gas station's garage, while Krantz unlatched the door and fell out of the Suzuki Samurai and into the snow. He got up and started running toward the field of snow. He was weak and he staggered; the handcuffs made movement awkward. He walked and ran. He was breathing heavily, and was experiencing a shortness of breath. He saw a farmhouse in the distance. He kept running toward the house, which was surrounded by some black and crippled trees. It was getting dark. He reached the farmhouse door which was hanging off its hinges. It creaked as he opened it. Three mice scurried across the floor. The small farmhouse was abandoned. He went inside and sat down at an old table. He laid his head on the table and went to sleep.

32

The little Pennsylvania town was swarming with scientists who were there to study a crater that had been apparently caused by an extraterrestrial impact. In a remote farmhouse, Krantz was asleep sitting at the table, his head resting on the surface. When he awoke he saw two creatures standing before him. He recognized them as aides to the people who had sent him on the journey. They were the interrogators, and before he could say anything they asked him the first question. They were dressed in skin-fitting suits which covered everything but their eyes and lips. One was dressed in black, the other white.

"Why did you pick a name like Krantz in the first place?"

"I dunno, I think that I saw it on a paperback in an airport bookstore," Krantz said, rubbing his eyes and yawning.

"Well, that was your first mistake, and then that episode with the cocaine," the black one continued.

"I was experimenting."

"And the conversion. You were only supposed to fake it, and then we caught you praying. Praying to one of their gods. The others wanted to eliminate you, but we overruled them," the white one said, glancing at the black one. Their voices sounded like those of cartoon chipmunks.

"We didn't do it because we thought you would come to your senses. Get over your addiction to things earthly, and concentrate on your mission."

"I didn't know that my life was in danger."

"Do you remember the night you remained late in the White House, that four years ago, and you were asking for a sign from one of their gods, a red-eyed monster came running down the hall at you?" the black one said.

"Yes, I remember. I thought that I was seeing things. I rushed out of the White House."

"It was Satan. He favors the image of the coyote. We didn't want you anymore and were about to send a substitute, but then we decided against it. We figured that just as you got over your coke addiction, you'd get over your Pentecostalism and your dreadful right-wing politics.

"Satan does work all over the universe. He collects souls like a homeless surp down here might collect bottles or cans. He does us a favor, sort of like what the algae does for the clam. Imagine what would happen if the devil didn't collect souls. The universe would be more cluttered than it is." The black one stared at the white one, who had a tendency to poeticize.

"Now they've put you out of the White House, and we can't find out what is going on," the black one said.

"And you're about to fall in love with a woman," the white one said.

"This love they have—it makes you feel good all over. We could use some of this back home. Everybody there is so businesslike. So abstract," Krantz said, moonily.

"He's fallen under their power," the black one said. "Maybe

we should remove him from this assignment. This love thing has led to nothing but misery on this planet. Wars, feuds. They've never been able to create a great civilization because of this . . . distraction. I mean I've read this Plato, Aristotle, Hegel, and all the rest. If those are the best minds that they could come up with, then they're better off blown to kingdom come. You can understand why they haven't advanced technologically. They spent the first thousand years of philosophy trying to decide whether matter was real or an illusion."

"We don't have time to train another one. All of the time and effort we've spent on him would be wasted. All he's learned about their habits and their ways of communicating," the white one said.

"This is the third one we've lost to them. There's something about this place. There's just so many things to do. So much to see," the black one said, in a sort of reverie. The white one gave him a reproachful glance. "Not that anything here can top what we have," the black one added quickly.

"Krantz, I know that it's easy to fall in love with this place, but you've forgotten what your original assignment was. Why you were sent here. The years you spent studying communications and nuclear weaponry. The barbarians are about to invade our planet. It's being taken over by the yellows. We blacks and whites have no place to go. You were supposed to start a little nuclear action here so that these cockroaches on two feet would be removed and there'd be room for us. But you've become sidetracked over such issues as loyalty and now love. Loyalty to Reverend Jones because he saved you from a burning sports car. And love for this woman," the white one said.

"I just don't think that I can betray Jones. He saved my life."

"That incident merely inflated what was already an overlarge ego," the black one said.

"But now he's turned against me. At one time, he was like a father to me. I've never met anybody as . . . as pure as he is. Sure, he has some crazy ideas, but all of the rest of the televangelists, with their theme parks and their constant whining for money, and their prostitutes and gay lovers, the wives and their mascara farms—Reverend Jones cleaned all of that up."

"He's responsible for the death of his mother. It's bound to come up sooner or later," the black one said.

"He what?"

"He hired an orderly to abuse her in a nursing home or something. Anyway, we checked him out," the white one said.

"Maybe that will cure you of your addiction to earthly habits. Phony. They're all scoundrels. Not one of them without larceny in his heart. The sooner we get rid of them the better," the white one said.

"Maybe you're right," Krantz said, stunned.

"Now you're beginning to see it our way," the black one said.

"We'll give you another chance. Pretty soon Jones will need all of the help he can get. Try to get to him. Offer your services," the white one said.

"What about Clift?"

"We'll take care of Clift," the black one said. He pulled a ray gun from the holster on his hip and vaporized the handcuffs that had been on Krantz's wrists. "Krantz, I hope that you will succeed this time. Try to get over your addiction to things earthly. We'll do something for this planet. Rejuvenate it. Look at what these people have done to it. Why, that ozone belt is about depleted. It will destroy all life on earth. If we get rid of these earthlings, we'll save the earth, before they finish it off."

"I hope you succeed, Krantz. If you don't, we plan to kidnap all of the American women and hold them hostage until these inferiors submit to our demands." Krantz laughed for about three minutes. The black one looked at the white one. They were puzzled as Krantz laughed until he eased out of the chair and began to roll about the floor, holding his stomach. "What's so funny?" they finally asked.

"Go and read Truman Capote, Tennessee Williams, and Edward Albee. You'll find out."

33

Though the Xmas advertising has sometimes shown Peter with as much sensitivity as a colon, he always answers a voice in distress. Just part of his nature. He really can't bring himself to be mean, and hasn't given a child a switch in hundreds of years. Besides, you switch a modern child, and they might have enough sense to dial 911 on your behind, or call some social worker to charge you with child abuse. He knew what everybody in the country knew. That Black Peter had been eclipsed by Saint Nicholas. Nicholas's material was larger, more global, and after the testimonies of James Way, the Social Darwinist columnist, who mixed up a little Skinner and Malthus in his theories, and Nola Payne, fifty-two Congressmen and just about half of Washington, Black Peter's miracles involving Tommy Turkey, Beechiko Mizuni, and Fryer Moog, plus a number of surps, and others at the bottom, didn't seem to amount to much in the public's eye. All that they did was to deter him from his mission. That of putting the impostor out of business, permanently. Little did Black Peter know that the ersatz Black Peter was out of business alright. He had been discarded like an old wind-up toy.

Jack Frost had the hotel change the locks on the door, and when he tried to phone Frost for an explanation, Frost was unavailable or "in conference." He read the *Wall Street Journal* the next day and got the explanation. There was a boom on Nick, and a bust on Peter. All of the prices on Black Peter's goods had been slashed drastically.

They always seem to be able to find each other, and so Peter went over to Saint Nicholas's earthly headquarters to wish him congratulations.

34

As he entered the compound where Saint Nicholas and his party were staying, he heard roaring laughter and drunken yells. It sounded like Geneva's old town on a Friday night. It was a Spanish-style house, and through the window he could see men and women dancing around a huge Xmas tree. The señoritas were playing the castanets, and the men had their hands behind their backs and seemed to be doing a dance which resembled one of tap dancing's ancestors. Men and women were wearing the heads of mice, to symbolize the animals which came with Nick and Peter from Spain. Peter made his way through the dozens of couples who'd come to get Nick to bless them with fertility. Nicholas was seated at the head of a long table; he had a huge barrel of wine to his lips and he was drinking it all down. It was like the party scene in Eisenstein's *Ivan the Terrible*, as each elf at the table was trying to keep up with Nicholas. Nicholas was known all over the ancient world for his garish appetites, which explains why his followers were condemned in the Book of Revelations. Peter knocked on the door. It was finally answered by Destar D'Nooza, an elf with an evil temper. He was frowning, but when he saw Pete, his black eyes glistened with merriment. "Well, look who is here, you lost dis time." Everybody turned toward the door. It became silent.

Nicholas stopped guzzling the wine. Pete walked in. He looked around the huge room which was covered with Xmas decorations: holly, ribbons, bows, poinsettias. In the middle of the feast was a wild boar with an apple in its mouth. There were huge bowls of fruit on the table, and before each guest was a Bernplatte, and a package of Rolaids. Tree lights. Stuffed stockings. Animal shaped cookies.

"Well, how do you like it, Pete?"

"You used to not go in for this kind of thing, Nick."

"One changes with the times, Pete. Maybe that's why I'm on the covers of all the magazines and you—"

"Look, I just came over to congratulate you. I thought what you did was marvelous. The Supreme Court Justice, the hard-boiled conservative newsman, and the others. I just don't see how you're going to be able to top that."

"I plan to." Nick turned to some of his chief elves and winked. "By the way. I heard that there was some impish person who was impersonating you, taking credit for all of your work. The fellow made a fortune, I understand. They said that you were angry, and were coming here to vanquish the unfortunate chap."

"Yeah. He was in way over his head. I got distracted, though."

"You always were a soft touch. I don't know how you got the reputation for being so mean and nasty. Why you were the one who was always handing out the gifts and going down the chimney, while all I did was sit on my ass and ride a white horse."

"So you finally acknowledge that."

"Why not? This Xmas has solidified my reputation. I can afford to be generous." Pete walked to the head of the table and shook hands with Nick. The elves and the guests applauded. Destar D'Nooza fumed. "Sure you won't have something to drink, or a bite to eat? There's plenty," Nick said. He was wearing a wreath of laurels which he always donned for special occasions. "Destar, get Pete a glass of wine."

"No, I think I'll be heading on back." D'Nooza was relieved.

"You mean you're not bitter? Jealous?" Nick said, rising, and removing a turkey drumstick from his mouth.

"Naw. Forget about it. The best man won. I don't have any excuses. Look at the turkey who was getting such a bad reputation from his classmate, the Japanese girl who wanted to be blonde, the musician who was dependent upon machines. He got back his chops. Certainly they were small, modest miracles, but they brought happiness to those people who experienced them. And what would have happened had I just returned to this place seeking revenge? History would have given me another black eye. No, I think I should be pleased with myself this season. Nick, you change the world; all I want to do is to help the little folk from time to time, individuals caught in situations that they can't seem to get out of."

Pete turned around and slowly walked out into the snow. As soon as he left the fiddle started up again, and the laughter and the drunken singing.

35

It was Xmas, and Nance had to leave his car in one of La Guardia's parking lots. He rode the bus to the subway to head toward home. On the train a man was sitting across from him. The man looked familiar. Nance kept staring at him, and the man, perhaps feeling that he was being stared at, awoke. He looked as though he hadn't shaved for days. His clothes were filthy, and a bruised knee was sticking out of a hole in his pants. His shoes lacked shoelaces, and he wasn't wearing socks. His ankles were ashen and bony. His hair was in dreds and it looked dirty, as though it were covered with white powder. He had cuts all over his face, and his lips were busted as though he'd been in a fight. His military jacket was in shreds. Black Peter leveled a defiant gaze at Nance Saturday. "Hey, Bro. Can you give a fellow a dollar or two for some Xmas soup? I haven't eaten today." Nance reached into his coat pocket and gave the man a five-dollar bill.

"You look familiar," Nance said.

"Yeah, you must have seen me in the newspapers."

"Black Peter. That's it. Boy, you sure did con your way up. I remember when you were with the ragtag band of

weirdos. If you guys only knew the trouble you caused me."
Nance looked the man up and down.

"I had it made there for a while. They gave me this suite
in a hotel and people waited on me, and satisfied my every
desire. Now they're backing Saint Nick."

"But you were acquiring such a good press. Helping those
people. Seems that your bosses would have liked that."

"That wasn't me who did all of that."

"If it wasn't you, then who was it?"

"I don't know. This Xmas sure has been spooky. You see
all of those people down in Washington testifying about seeing
Saint Nick. Talking about cutting the defense budget. Universal health care and free day care, cradle-to-grave security
like they got in those socialist countries." Evidence of Nick's
success was immediately above their heads. There were ads
showing Nick smiling next to products. Pete's billboards had
been taken down and his ads removed from the newspapers.

"Next year's an election year, they're liable to say anything,
but it would be terrific if it were true. But this stuff about
Saint Nicholas and the miracles. That's crazy. I hear that
Nola Payne was an alcoholic. She was probably having the
d.t.'s when she said she saw Saint Nicholas. But never mind
all of that—I want you to tell me where I went wrong. Why
I couldn't find Snow Man."

"Snow Man?"

"Yeah, Snow Man, the one that Joe Baby hired to kill Boy
Bishop. I've spent sleepless nights wondering where I went
wrong.

"They killed an intruder and then brought him back to
life. They used the water from Tarpon Springs, Florida. They
said that the water is what kept him alive. They had me throw
my voice into his corpse—I mean, he was like a zombie.

They dressed him up like Santa Claus and used him to make speeches against the people who were making money off Xmas. They made me do it, and they kidnapped the real Santa Claus that this company had bought, and substituted the dead body of this gangster," Peter said, eyeing Nance, trying to determine whether this story was convincing to him.

"Gangster? What did he look like?"

"The man came busting into this place they had, but one of Boy Bishop's bodyguards killed him. He was on the heavy side."

"They killed him. I knew it. I figured that something like that happened." Nance was so excited that he jumped up from where he was seated next to Black Peter. The next stop on the subway was Broadway–Lafayette. He remembered that Jamaica Queens lived in Soho. He was so excited that he didn't know what to do and had missed his stop. He got up and headed toward the subway door.

"People are always using me, getting me into trouble, making me do things that I don't want to do, putting me up to things—Sir?" Nance looked back at Peter, now sobbing, tears running down his cheeks.

"Yes, what is it?"

"You wouldn't happen to have five more bucks, would you? I feel like calling my mom. After all, it's Xmas, ain't it?" Nance gave him another five dollars. He got off the subway. He hadn't felt this good in a few years. He told the first person he saw to have a Merry Xmas.

36

"How did you do that?" Jones said.

"With the help of my Lord and Master," Lucy Artemis said, putting her fingers to her lips. She whistled, and out of a puff of smoke that startled Reverend Jones appeared a man who was dressed like a dandy. He had a face shaped like a big egg. He was dressed in a cream-colored double-breasted suit, pink shirt with pearl cuff links, a tie with the print of some show-off flower, and black and white faux spats. Reverend Jones had seen his picture in a *Washington Sun* book review, and recognized him as a stage Irishman of the sort who used to black up to entertain WASPs with jokes about blacks and Jews. Lucy Artemis beamed, while Reverend Jones seemed puzzled.

"My Lord and Master, you're such a prince when it comes to disguises," Lucy said. Satan promised her that he would take her out of the homeless shelter if she supplied him with the soul of a powerful person, and Satan had kept his part of the bargain. She was wearing an outfit she'd bought from Neiman Marcus with the money that Satan had advanced her. There was a lot of money rolling around hell. She was as black as her followers at Esephus had painted her, and she wore bright hellfire lipstick. She'd go back into the soothsaying business and call on all of her clients, Congressmen, Senators, now that she and Reverend Jones were allies.

"Yeah, part of the contract is that I get to use the tropes of my clients from time to time. I decided to use this novelist who wanted a best-seller, and was really desperate. I gave the son of a bitch a contract though I have so many conventional novelists in hell, anyway. I'm more of a Ray Federman man, myself," Satan said, in a grousing, gravelly baritone voice. "He doesn't give a shit about characters, nor do I; he leaves their souls to me." *Beepbeepbeepbeepbeepbeepbeep.* Somebody was paging Satan. He took a beeper out of his suit coat pocket. "He what . . . look you tell that bastard Jefferson Davis that I'm not bringing back a twist of lime for his julep. Hell is not a country club."

"You know Reverend Jones?" Lucy asked.

"Yes, I know the man. Another one of these Christian hypocrites. As if we didn't have enough in the eighties. That Swaggart and the Bakkers. Well, at least this one is interesting."

"I resent that. I don't smoke, I don't drink, and I keep my britches down—I mean, up," Jones said.

"Yes, but I've heard your sermons, that is when you preached. Mercifully you don't do that anymore. You ever wonder why you always concentrated on the human sacrifice, incest, rape, cannibalism parts of the Bible? Deep down in your soul there's a pool of vomit and green pus. And by the way, what's the big idea of you going around telling the press that you've met me? I don't know you from Adam. I detest you, but I could use a man like you," Satan said.

"You can't bend my will. I'm a man of God, I'm bringing a Christian nation—"

"You locked your mother up for twenty days until she died of malnutrition, you didn't want to spend money on nursing homes, and when they found her, the ninety-year-old's bones were sticking out, she had bed sores all over her. *Jr., what you did to me was so cruel and heartless, Jr. how could you do that, wasn't it bad enough that you took the ax to my pet cat?*" Satan began speaking in the voice of Reverend Jones's late mother, whose death had been attributed to natural causes. Jones's fishing buddy in the coroner's office was now dead; he didn't think anybody knew. Jones began sobbing and bellowing like a baby bull.

"Who told you that—"

"Don't worry, I won't say anything. Some of my customers have done much worse. I got Abraham Lincoln down there."

"What? Abraham Lincoln? What did he do? What could he have possibly done?"

"I have a professional relationship with my clients and never discuss their cases."

"I'm not doing business with you."

"You want to hold on to power, don't you? I'll handle Clift."

"I don't know."

"I have references." Reverend Jones put on his glasses and looked through some of the contracts that had been signed by Thomas Jefferson, who credited Satan with being the coarchitect of the manifest destiny. Other names from antiquity to modern times also appeared. Jones was shocked at some of the names he read. Lucy and Satan smiled at each other. Satan flashed an image to the wall. It was Reverend

Jones in a prison cell, and some other prisoners were struggling with him, and trying to pull down his trousers. They were inner-city types, and they were grinning. Reverend Jones lost his composure.

Reverend Jones put on his glasses and examined the contract, his hands shaking.

"What? Why, I can't do that. Heinrich is my closest companion," he said, after reading the clause requiring Heinrich to return to hell. Hitler was lonely.

"We don't want him up here anymore. You need advisors who are more contemporary. We want to get rid of Heinrich, he's going back with me. As for that Joe Beowulf, that contraption, before the week is over I want that thing on a scrap heap in the D.C. dump. What good is it? One of my microbiologists is sending you one of these laboratory beings. He'll be much more efficient. It's time you entered the new century, shit, in a few years it'll be the year 2000. Microbiologists, deconstructionists, New Age freaks; I'm thinking about opening a new area called Jargon City which is where I'm going to put these new sinners. Sometimes I don't understand what they're talking about."

"But—"

"You'll do what I say. And I want you to stop this crazy thing you have about black people. I don't want any more of them in hell. They're always organizing protests and begging for air-conditioners. They're worse than the Jews."

"I don't know what you're talking about, Satan."

"You don't know what I'm talking about." Satan walked over to behind the desk and grabbed Reverend Jones's nose. "Ouuuuucccchhh," Reverend Jones said as Satan lifted the tubby man from his chair by the nose. Lucy cackled. Her new dentures fit fine. They cost ten thousand dollars, and she could eat fried turkey again, a recipe she learned in Nashville.

"Don't try to fool me, you son of a bitch. I know that you and these others have had a contingency plan to put blacks and the other surps in camps, like you did the Japs back there in World War II. You and these other fake Aryan loonies believe that they're my children. Well, I want to set the record straight. They're not. They're none of my kin. You keep them. I don't want any more of them. Some days they worry me so that I want to open peace talks with the other side. Why do you think I have to dress this way? The blacks tricked me out of all my attributes; my tail, my horns, they took the red off of my hide, and the Jews, they're always demanding things. I was talking to one of those Czars the other day and he said that out of the million Jews he had in Russia at one time, 999,999 were revolutionaries. Now look, Jones, I don't have all day. The way you're heading you're going straight to hell, but if you play along with the program you can linger for a while. I'll make you the most powerful man in America. You preach as good as a nigger, even though you don't have their *langage*. I stay away from these black churches. These black preachers do the gospel so well that I almost want to jump and shout myself. Last time I visited one, I almost marched up to be saved with the rest of the sinners, but that's no good. If I went over to the other side, there would be no symmetry in the world. Besides, one day I'll get my due from history. History will give the devil his due. I'm down here in the world hustling my ass off for souls, and he gets all of the devotion and credit. Nobody's even heard from him in thousands of years. It isn't fair," Satan said, staring at the ceiling. Satan let go of the Reverend's nose. Jones signed the contract.

"This calls for a toast," Lucy Artemis said.

The devil ran his hand across the table and three glasses of champagne appeared. The three drank from the glasses. When he finished his drink, the devil turned into a coyote and disappeared through a wall. Outside the door, Joe Beowulf stood. A synthetic tear came to his eye. Reverend Jones didn't want him, Hollywood didn't want him. What good was he, he thought.

37

When Artemis heard the familiar tinkle of the bell that preceded all of Nick's appearances, she winked at Reverend Jones
from where she stood behind the curtain. Sure enough Nick
suddenly appeared before Jones. The Saint whose persuasive
powers were so good that he put the devil on his payroll. The
Saint who influenced an Emperor of Rome, and now a President of the United States.

"You're not startled." Nick should have known something
was wrong then and there, because when he appeared they
usually became afraid. Some even got to their knees and
prayed.

"What's on your mind, Nick, I don't have all day."

"But . . . I well, I guess you've seen the Congressmen on
television, confessing to their sins, redeeming themselves,
making promises to do something, and the Mayor of New
York, Kevin Grouch, down in Tompkins Square Park, wash-
ing the feet of pan-handlers, and the Governor of California
—whatever you call the chap—both of them out there singing Xmas carols at orphan homes—Jones, you must show
that kind of leadership also." But Jones didn't even look up.

He kept making as though he were signing papers. Nick was shocked that his appearance didn't surprise Jones. He usually scared the bejesus out of people.

"If anybody's going to do the changing, you will," Jones said, still not looking up.

"Hello, Nick, baby." Nick turned around, and standing behind him was Lucy Artemis.

"But—"

"Yes, you thought you'd finished me off when you and your vulgar followers burned my beautiful temple. But I wasn't there that day. I was in the woods, hunting boars to sacrifice. I've hunted you down through history, and when I heard that you came to Washington a few winters back, I came and settled here." Nick tried to respond but his powers were frittering away. He was becoming dizzy. The room began to swirl. Before he blacked out, he heard Jones's and Artemis's laughter.

38

There were still a lot of odd-looking people living in Soho, but unlike in the late 60s it now reminded one of a campus with lonely young people staring out the windows of bars and restaurants. There were still galleries in which art hung that was less interesting than the jargon that was peddled in its behalf. Since the period of the modernists, art increasingly came to rely on an apparatus as large as General Motors in order for it to be successful. Jamaica Queens had quit journalism for acting, and was making quite a career of it, landing roles in Shakespeare and Ibsen. He yelled up at her loft. She opened the window and looked down at him. She didn't seem pleased to see him, but she threw down the keys. He opened the door and took the elevator to the fourth floor. The elevator opened on the loft, which she decorated with money from a blind trust that was located in Togo. She was standing there with a towel wrapped around her head. She was wearing a short bathrobe with what she called cubistic design. It looked Navajo to him. The loft was huge and had an upstairs where she slept. She was one of these people who haunted the flea markets for bargains, and so the place was full of junk.

"Nance, I'm not really in the mood for company." He could tell that she'd been crying.

"But when I saw you at the U.N. you said to drop down if I was ever in the neighborhood. I just got some good news. I wanted to share it with someone, besides you said you wanted to tell me about the invasion of Dominica."

"O, Nance, I'm sorry—it's just that I—" She walked up to him and put her arms around his neck. He could feel her heart beating through her robe. At that moment, he was glad he'd become celibate.

"Why don't I get you some eggnog, and you can tell me about it." She went into the kitchen. He was sitting on some Italian leather white sofa. He glanced at the Xmas tree she had in the corner, and the bright packaged presents underneath. On another wall was a Shango mask. It was made of wood, berries, mirrors, and cowrie shells. She was particularly pleased with this piece and talked about it. She came into the room and sat next to him.

"I just thought you needed a job. You know the last time I saw you you were a private detective."

"I never got a license."

"I was down in Dominica covering the invasion. What a joke that was."

"Joke? I thought that General Scott defeated the communist forces there. He was elected President on that rightwing ticket that was supposed to have been a change in direction from the drift toward the left begun with the Reagan admin—"

"Yes, that's what they say. But actually they only uncovered one communist, and he turned out to be on the C.I.A.'s payroll."

"What?"

"They didn't realize it until the Marines shot up his hotel room."

"But what about the combat footage?"

"It was manufactured by Towers Bradhurst, the man who invented Joe Beowulf. It wasn't even shot in Dominica. It was filmed in Marin County in California."

"Son of a bitch," Nance said. "Why didn't the press expose it?" Nance thought of what he had said, and they both laughed. "So is that what you wanted to tell me about the invasion?"

"No. I met these Rastas down there and they said they would pay $250,000 to anyone who would retrieve something that the Vatican had of theirs. Some sort of scepter-like object with a gold star on the top of carved wood. They said that it represents power over the nations of the world. Interested?"

"I don't know about going back in the detective business. Besides, a lot of these Rastas are fake. They're dumping crack into the ghettos. They had my neighborhood tweaked out until I snitched on their operations."

"You can't judge all Rastafarians by Black Peter and those who hang out on the beaches all over the Caribbean, smoking ganja and committing small crimes. There are bad Catholics, Buddhists, everywhere there's religion there are con artists and mack men.

"So what's the good news?" she finally said.

"You remember the first time we met?"

"Yes, you were searching for some man. You were on a job."

"Well, I just ran into Black Peter on the subway—"

"But the toy manufacturers gave him a big limousine. What's he doing on a subway?"

"They got rid of him since Nick is back. He's in a terrible mess. Looks as though he hasn't bathed in days. Has that surp smell."

"You don't believe all of that stuff, do you? Nola Payne. The turkey, and Fryer Moog. Jim Way and all of those Congressmen. It's all of that cocaine that they're dumping into the country. Everybody is seeing things and scratching themselves. Everybody is so hyper. Paranoid."

"Black Peter told me that his friends killed Snow Man."

"That gangster Joe Baby hired you to find?"

"Yeah. You see, I didn't fail at all. Of course the jive turkey made up some kind of story about a zombie, and the walking dead, but I figured he must have been on drugs or something. I had to give him ten dollars so that he could call his mother and buy a bite to eat." She was laughing.

"What's wrong."

"I haven't heard anybody say 'jive turkey' in so long."

She kept laughing. "Did you hear what Virginia said about you on television today?"

"No, what did she say?"

"She said that you were a boring lover. That you were a meat and potatoes man while she was the kind who liked to have an appetizer or a cocktail first. She said you always headed right for the main course." Nance got up to leave.

"Nance, I didn't mean—"

"Skip it. Nobody can bring me down tonight. It's Xmas. I'm starting life with a new slate. I was depressed since the T.T. Xmas over not being able to locate that guy, Snow Man. Now, thanks to Black Peter, I know that he's dead. That's a good feeling." He started out. He heard someone cough. He looked up and saw the Latin man climbing down the ladder which led to the second floor of her loft. He was just wearing a pair of shorts. Nance looked at Jamaica. She lowered her eyes. Nance headed for the elevator door. She rushed after him.

"Nance, you don't understand. He's mean, but he also has a good side. I can help him, Nance. I made him stop many of his bad habits. I mean, for example, he doesn't execute whole families anymore. Just the family member he's mad with."

"Señor," the man said, reeling about on the polished wood floors, a glass of wine in his hand. "When are we going to have our duel?"

"There's not going to be any duel," Nance said.

"Ah ha. Just as I thought. *Cobarde.*"

Nance entered the elevator. The man was standing there and Jamaica had her hand to her head. She was telling him to shut up. He kept calling Nance a *cobarde*. As the elevator descended, he still heard the man yell *cobarde*, and Jamaica say shut up. Then he heard a hard slap and a scream. Outside he walked past some carolers. They were singing a song about Joseph, the father of Jesus. He'd never heard of this song. He wondered did Joseph ever get into any duels or brawls. He wondered was Joseph somewhere right now thinking: Here I am, god's stepfather, and all I get out of the deal is one song. I worked and saved, and paid my taxes, and took a lot of lip from this smartass kid too, whom his mother was devoted to more than to me, and ridicule from all of the guys for falling for that story about immaculate conception. I still think the butcher did it. Mary had a taste for lamb. Always had to take my meals after the family pets got theirs. Nobody even said, why thank you, Joseph, for raising this kid and giving him food and shelter.

39

When Nance entered the apartment the telephone was ringing. He picked it up. Long distance. Italy. He didn't know anybody in Italy. They said to stand by for Cardinal Malidori. Cardinal who?

"Mr. Saturday, Nance Saturday?"

"You got him," Nance said.

"I know that you're a busy man, but if I could prevail upon you to lend some assistance to my organization. We would be eternally grateful to you, and—"

"Slow down. What organization, who are you?"

"Malidori is my name, and I'm calling from Italy."

"How did you get my name?" He mentioned one of his former clients. She was really in a bad way, behind in her credit card payments—she owed over one hundred thousand dollars—her rent, not to mention the clothing, cosmetic surgery, and utility bills, and had nothing but a piece of Kraft cheese in her refrigerator until he straightened things out for her. Now she was in Italy and had embarked on a successful modeling career. He said that he'd read about his help to her in an Italian newspaper. That she'd always given him credit for getting rid of her debts so that she could make a new start. Malidori said that he was working with a man who was so obsessed with Satan that he threatened the survival of an organization that was almost two thousand years old. An organization that was two thousand years old must have accumulated a lot of assets, Nance thought. When the man told him how much his organization was willing to pay for his services, Nance imagined himself at La Guardia, reading the newspapers and checking his watch as his fleet of old black Cadillacs, driven by his drivers, made the trip back and forth from the shuttle to downtown hotels.

"When do you want me to start?" Nance asked.

"Your ticket is at the Pan Am ticket counter," the man said.

After the man hung up, Nance thought about how his luck had changed during the course of the day. He had begun the day feeling like Boston, that day in 1987 after both the Celtics and Marvin Hagler lost. But now he felt like Scrooge must have felt after his long night of the soul, a character in the novel by the English novelist whose last name, Dickens, was a variation of the name Nicholas. And while he was in Rome, he could see what he could do to locate the Rastafarian scepter. Two hundred and fifty thousand dollars was a lot of cash. He saw himself in the yellow pages: Nance Saturday's Limousine Service.

40

Unlike the part of that nebulous world, the Netherlands, where Nick dwelled, where at least there were some elves to do the entertaining, the atmosphere of this exclusive club was always disciplined and austere. There being no such thing as black-tie optional here, the men were standing about in tuxedos. They could have been models in a Ralph Lauren ad. They all wore the pout that had become an image of the nasty 80s. Though they were, like Nick, at one time as dark as vanilla extract, they had been whitened over the years; as white as the fence that Tom Sawyer, the trickster, got his fellows to paint. This board of directors of eleven were waiting for their chairman, Saint Peter, to arrive. Their founder— as pale as a rock cod—could be seen in a portrait, in which he appeared as unshaven as in the Dali painting of the same subject.

When Saint Peter arrived, they all completed their cocktails and took their places in love seats and sofas which were as black and curvaceous as a Porsche. They had that Italian look, and were as elegant as a mosquito. He told them that Nick had gotten into trouble with his old nemesis, Lucy

Artemis, still mad because he destroyed her temple and seduced her followers. That his vanity had again done him in, and not willing to quit while he was ahead, having altered the course of American history, he pushed his luck and got involved with one of Satan's new customers, Reverend Clement Jones, a charlatan who'd gained power in the United States, where the public opinion was fickle and Piscean. All of the Saints were aware of America's Attention Deficit Disorder which permitted only one image to reign at a time, and only briefly, before being replaced by another. Though he knew their disdain for this renegade Saint, who in the Middle Ages rivaled Mary in popularity, he was still one of theirs and they'd have to get him out of a jam, even if it meant calling on the services of Black Peter. A couple of Saints sighed at the mention of Black Peter. A vote was taken. Six for, five against, and one abstention. A grim Saint Peter sent a message home to Guinea, the island beneath the Caribbean.

41

Peter was glad to be back home in Guinea. He had gone to excise the impostor, Black Peter, from history, but, as usual, forgot his mission and ended up doing good deeds. He would leave global politics to Nick. He could have it. Xmas in the world had been troubled as usual. Bethlehem had been shut off to outsiders because of gunplay between competing religions. The dollar was chasing the yen like Tom the cat chasing Jerry the mouse.

Black Peter was reclining on a rock which was shaped like the head of a rhino. Crabs were crawling in and out of holes and in the distance French bathers, two women with billiard ball buttocks and a man wearing Ray Bans, were wading into the Caribbean, accompanied by their black dog. Black Peter was sitting under a palm tree, cooking a pot of blood sausage for his friend, the mosquito, who couldn't wait to lay his proboscis upon it.

"You seem more relaxed than I ever seen you," said Mosquito in his high-pitched, wiry voice.

"Glad to be back home."

"But Black Peter, the impostor. Your original purpose was to put him out of business."

"I did. The toy manufacturers thought that it was he who was helping all of those people. The Turkey, Beechiko, Fryer Moog, and the others. And so Nick, knowing that I was behind the whole thing, decided to get into that metaphysical arm wrestling contest that he likes to get into with me, upstaged my work. The toy manufacturers got rid of Peter, and are now promoting Nick's image again. You know how fickle market forces are. Economics has about as much sense as a tornado. Besides, I'm tired of the competition. I went and congratulated Nick."

"You did what?"

"I congratulated him. It's bad enough that history views me as a lackey and a buffoon, but not a poor loser as well."

"Now you're talking, Bro Peter. Once you get a bad rap, it's hard to shake it off. Hell, in my family there are two thousand species. We got folks around in the arctic. I don't even bite. But everybody thinks that all of us are responsible for yellow fever and malaria," the mosquito said.

"Well, at least the impostor is out of business. Always trying to scam somebody or put something over on somebody. But with the toy manufacturers, he met his match. Once they use you up, they go out and get somebody else. Now he's hoboing around on the subway. Probably end up back on Broadway with his dummy act. Clever fellow; if he tried to channel his energy into something useful, he'd benefit mankind." Bro Mosquito drew some liquid from the blood sausage.

"Hummm-hum! Peter, you know how to cook some blood sausage alright. You and Nick ought to stop your bizarre relationship. You seem to need each other. You feed off each other. It's strange."

"The competition is over. Look, I'll never convince the people in those cold climates that I'm the one who does all of the dirty work for Nick."

"I'd forget about it if I were you. Forget about it." Firecrackers were going off. They could hear the band in the distance. It was Shango's day, and so they were playing Tchaikovsky's 1812 Overture. Bro Turtle was ponderously making his way toward the pair. There was a telephone on his shell. Peter picked it up. He listened.

"I'll be right there."

"Where you going, Bro Peter?" the turtle and the mosquito asked simultaneously.

"It's the Saints. Nick's in trouble. I got to go." And with that, Black Peter was off.

One of the old ones shambled up on the beach. It was Bro Lobster. The ancient crustacean must have weighed one, two hundred, he must have weighed at least five hundred pounds. They stood out of respect, because here was one among them who was there at the creation. He knew all of the stories.

"What say, Bro Lobster?" they said, greeting the lobster who was scrambling up on the beach in a jerking fashion as the tide played with his body. His many legs moved slowly.

"Hello, Bro Mosquito and Bro Turtle. What you boys up to? O, and happy Shango Day."

"Happy Shango Day to you, Bro Lobster," they both said together.

"Wasn't that Bro Peter who just flew out of here?"

They nodded their heads. Turtle was munching on some

of the fish that Bro Peter had left in the skillet being kept hot by a low flame; it was making a sizzling sound.

"Boy, is he complicated, or should I say, they," the lobster said.

"What do you mean, Bro Lobster?"

"Yeah. Tell us?" Bro Mosquito said.

"Well, you know, Bro Peter and Bro Nick are the same person. They were a King some hundreds of years ago in a Yoruban kingdom, and once a year the King was required to throw a feast at which he would give all of the members of his village gifts. Wan't no war, or drought, or plague or any of those things in those days. Hey, what you got there, Bro Mosquito?" the lobster, whom everybody called Das Alte, said.

"It's some of that white rum that Black Peter likes so much." The lobster reached out a pincer and sampled a taste of the rum.

"Anyway, one year a stranger showed up to the village. He demanded to have a gift, too, but the King refused, and the stranger went away, but not before warning the King that he'd regret it. Shortly after he left, the people began to die, and the King went to Ela, who told him that the stranger was Death, and that, for insulting the stranger, he was responsible for the advent of death in the world. It all came down to a matter of give and take. Death takes. I don't know much about Peter's career except that he shows up in Spain in the Middle Ages and is covered over with some Christian figure, underneath which is a matriarch of early Turkey associated with tree worship. Then he's split into white and black along the way. The main thing is that he has to give gifts because he feels that some day he will meet up with Death, and Death will accept his gift. Then he thinks that

Death will come to an end in the world. A foolish quest if you ask me."

"But, Bro Lobster, how can Nick and Peter, who are opposites, be the same?" the turtle asked. But the lobster wasn't saying.

The sun was the color of the lobster's coat. The palm trees began to sway. A dog barked in the distance. Soon it was dark, and the lobster, mosquito, and turtle relaxed, staring up at a ship, in the distance, moving across the ocean of sky. They wondered what its destination was. And then the sky was filled with shattered lights as the fireworks began, and the cannons began to be fired as Shango's music, the 1812 Overture, was coming to an end.

42

As Clift's caravan of black cars headed through the gates of
the sanatorium toward the highway that would take them
into the nation's capital, the well-wishers cheered; Clift waved
to them as they lined the road leading to the highway. There
was only one dissenter, and he was from the D'Roaches,
those who believed that cockroaches would make an appro-
priate food supply after a nuclear war, and he held aloft the
symbol of the D'Roaches, the computer-generated image of
the androgynous Leonardo Da Vinci. John was in the second
car, seated next to Jack Marshall, the car's driver; the press
and Secret Service agents were driving behind. Clift had
gained about fifteen pounds and his hair was greyer. He had
lost the face that had graced the cover of thousands of fashion
magazines. He had spent the three years reading, something
he hadn't had time for since he began his career in modeling.
He was also able to invite some of the nation's writers, schol-
ars, intellectuals, workers, and students to visit him during
his "rest," as the Hatch administration called his virtual imprisonment. He had read avidly of the world's literature: from
Africa, Asia, India, Afro-America, and he had also talked to

many of the contemporary authors and intellectuals from around the world. His speech would quote from the world's literature as well as from the Bible, which, in his view, had been exploited by televangelists and fundamentalists over the years. He could imagine Christ, armed as he was when he chased the moneylenders from the temple, flogging the TV evangelists until they fled their pulpits. Jones invoked the sinister side of the scriptures, while in his speech Clift had decided that he would quote the sections about the poor and about peace.

He didn't know whether he'd want to live in the White House. Maybe it was time to build something that didn't look like a set from *Gone with the Wind*. He'd worked on his speech all night. A speech setting the tone for the Clift administration—the unfinished administration that had been aborted when he'd gone on television and announced that St. Nick had revealed to him the off-the-shelf operation: the Terrible Twos, but now everybody in Washington believed him. Thanks to the Admiral's letter, and Nola Payne, James Way, and a score of Congressmen.

The passengers in the black limousine rode in silence, as the procession rolled through the Maryland winter toward Washington.

Suddenly, the motorcycle escort which preceded Clift's car stopped. There was a black Winnebago up ahead. It was blocking the road. One of the policemen waved his hand at the driver, a signal for the van to move. Shots were fired from the Winnebago.

43

Weary of waiting in the cold, the marching bands had left hours before. The huge disappointed crowds that had been gathered in a cold and rainy downtown Washington to greet Dean Clift and his party had also dispersed. They had spent hours rubbing and blowing into their hands for warmth. The workmen were dismantling the platforms upon which Dean Clift, flanked by those Congressmen who were not members of the New Christian majority, was to make his first speech since the Supreme Court declared his ouster from office under the disability amendment unconstitutional. The bulletin had been carried by the networks that evening, announcing that Clift's motorcade had vanished on its way to Washington. John was sitting in his chair. He was so depressed that he couldn't finish his Xmas meal. The TV news crew that came to record his eyewitness to the disappearance of Dean Clift and his party had packed up and left. His nephew was sitting across from him. His nephew was in fifth grade, and earning all A's. He had grown accustomed to his artificial limb, and was a merry young lad with bushy hair and long, strong arms. He had baby eyes like Jesse Jackson.

"Can I get you something?" Esther asked. Jane was in the kitchen, preparing the Xmas meal. Esther shook her head slowly. Both of them wore black glossy wigs over their grey hair, and between the pensions their husbands left and their White House salaries, they eked by.

"John, it wasn't your fault that the President disappeared," Esther said.

"But only if I had sat in the front car with him, it never would have happened."

"Uncle John, this fight is bigger than you. President Clift has some powerful people mad at him. We studied it in current affairs at school. People didn't want him to return to Washington," his grandson said. He reminded him of his mother, John's daughter, who had been killed in a car crash. Had her nose, and his son-in-law's mouth. John hoped that he could stay alive until he was eighteen. He hoped he could live with his irregular heartbeat.

"I'll bet that Reverend Jones had something to do with it," John said.

Jane came into the kitchen and joined the conversation. "He ordered everybody to get his things packed, and I understand that they had a ticket for him on Piedmont Airlines, then after he spent some time with that crazy woman, what's her name?"

"Lucy Artemis. She's that woman that all of those Congressmen go to. Some kind of fortune-teller. She's the one who said that America was going to be taken over by some kind of snake religion," Esther said.

John usually looked forward to these Xmas dinners with Esther and Jane. They'd usually have a fine time discussing their days in the White House where Esther and Jane still worked. He had only picked at his food. That morning was supposed to have been the end of the Terribles. Dean Clift would arrive into the Capitol and pick up where he'd left off. That speech he had made during the Xmas of the Terrible Twos. The one that had raised the hopes of so many millions of people.

"I hear they were all in there laughing. That German soldier, Lucy Artemis, and others," Jane said. "What do you mean, others?" John said. "And I thought that this German soldier, Heinrich, the one they were supposed to have brought back from Bitburg—I thought that he was a figment of Jones's imagination."

"We heard him. Jane saw him." John turned to Jane.

"You're making that up," he said. Jane crossed herself.

"I swear fo' God. It was late one night at the White House. I had to stay late because Ms. Hatch was hosting a dinner. Well, she was so full of Valium that she got the shakes. Started giggling and acting inappropriate and talking a lot. It took me a while to get her to bed, and I was about to leave when I saw this soldier, standing in the hall. I thought it was one of the guards, but then I saw the helmet and the man look like he didn't have no black in his eyes, you know, look like his eyes were white, and he smelled real bad. He smell the way dead people smell. One of the drivers said that he had seen him too. Said it was that old Nazi, Heinrich, whose spirit Ronald Reagan, the man who used to be in the White House, brought back from some Nazi cemetery. Well, he didn't actually bring him back, the man stowed away, or his spirit stowed away." The wood was sending up sparks in the fireplace. Esther came in and poured glasses of whiskey all around. The grandchild was under the Xmas tree, playing with his toys.

"They said on the news that Reverend Jones and Jesse

Hatch and them were holding meetings to decide what to do next. They're trying to get their friends in Congress to give them power until Clift can be found. Said that everybody is out looking for Clift. That's a laugh," John said. His voice was touched by bitterness and disgust.

"Grandpa, what happens if they can't find him? Does that mean that Jesse Hatch can still be President?" John didn't respond.

"Soon as it was announced that Clift had disappeared the plane that Jesse Hatch was on turned around and headed back to Washington," Esther said. "I'll bet Vice President Scabb is happy. He wants to run."

"Ain't he the one responsible for all that crack and heroin coming into the country?" Jane said.

"Nobody knows. The press is afraid of him. He's been the head of a lot of secret organizations in the government," John said.

"What do you make of all of these people seeing Saint Nicholas? Just drunk?" Esther started to laugh.

"You should see the way Reverend Jones be rehearsing his preaching. Say he has to be in shape for his return to the pulpit when his mission to save America is through. He's always listening to Reverend Franklin's sermons and watching videos of Al Green, James Brown, and picking up pointers. Sometimes he take the rug off the floor and starts practicing sliding across the pulpit and doing splits," Jane said. They laughed. "Said that when he returns to preaching he's going to get a drummer like them Pentecostals use."

"When are the Terribles going to end?" John finally said.

"Reverend McBee said that the Terribles will afflict America till she quits her wicked ways. That America's Babylon and that Babylon will fall," said Esther.

"Hey, why's everybody so serious? This is supposed to be a day of joy and celebration," John said, trying to manage a smile.

They kept drinking and talking, and telling stories about the old days, and gossiping. The grandchild was underneath the Xmas tree talking to his doll. His Black Peter doll.

44

On Christmas Day, the *Washington Sun*'s front page carried the following stories:

The Haitian maid released the late Admiral Matthew's letter. Her lawyer said that she had left her country because her religion, a religion of the people, had been abused by the unscrupulous elite to punish their enemies instead of being used to heal and to give every peasant godlike powers, and that a jingoistic inner circle had fought against the restoration of democratic values. She had grown fond of the United States and didn't want the same thing to happen here. She didn't want the United States to become Big Haiti where the Bill of Rights was trampled by men in touch with the negative forces of the heart, and didn't want an off-the-shelf operation consisting of oligarchs to rule in the name of democracy. She said that the release of this letter was her Xmas present to her new fellow citizens.

Dear (Name illegible)

You know that I'm a stand-up guy for my country. Hell, everytime I see old glory go by I break out in

goose pimples. And so when the old man, General
Walter Scott, invited me to join his administration,
I stopped what I was doing, put my money in a blind
trust and me and the missus took off for Washington
on the first flight available. Though alot of his enemies said that that invasion of Dominica was staged
so that his party would win the election, it made me
proud to be an American again. It was a recovery
from the sellout of Central America by the Bolshevik
100th Congress and that left-winger Reagan's peace
treaty with the Russians at Reykjavik, the greatest
betrayal since that crippled son of a bitch Roosevelt
gave eastern Europe to the commies at Yalta. I wouldn't
have joined anybody else because in my opinion the
Washington politician is in the same category as those
leeches the grunts used to suffer in Vietnam. You
know how I felt about that war. If they'd left that war
to the navy we would have won. A few warheads
launched from underneath the sea outside of Hai-
phong harbor would have done the job. Nuked Ho
Chi Minh and his crowd to kingdom come. You
know what Ike said. Asians haven't the slightest regard
for life anyway, so nuking them would have been
like mashing a bunch of ants. But the Harvard and
Yale educated bastards in Washington were holding
us back.

It was the army that lost Korea, and if it hadn't
been for the reds, the army would have lost World
War II as well. If it wasn't for the navy and the air
force guys, the Japs would have invaded the United
States and we'd all be working for them by now.

I'll tell you, they had some weird characters in the

White House. There was this Vice President Dean Clift—the guy was so dumb that I don't think he knew what century he was born into. They only put him up as vice president because the old man wanted to close the gender gap by putting up somebody with a pretty face. It worked. Soon as the selection was announced the broads opened their legs and lubricated. The old man's advisors were right. All they had to do was put Clift's face on their night tables, and the women would forget about the old man's promise to charge all women guilty of having abortions with murder, and his threat to place all feminists under house arrest, which is the way it was before the nineteen sixties.

The Scott/Clift ticket went up 15% in the polls from the women's vote, leaving the traitor commie big-spending flag-burning scum on the other ticket in the dust. Just goes to show that women think with their cunts.

The King of Beer. This guy was also plainly nuts, and was always sidling into Washington on his private plane late at night. He thought that the Indians had put a curse on him for violating some sacred spring. But the scariest of them all was Reverend Clement Jones. He was one of these premillenarians, I think you call them. Talked all the time about the rapture or some such thing having to do with the end of the world. He had some influence over old man Scott who was ninety years old when they elected him.

My wife hated Jones. He once asked her to leave a reception for wearing too much makeup. You know, she used to be a show girl, but that part of her life

is behind her. He's lucky we were *in* the White House.
I started to floor the bastard. This son of a bitch was
out of his mind, and he had brought a kid named
Bob Krantz in with him, a kid with a lot of likeability,
but he didn't always seem in possession of himself,
as though his mind were a million miles away. The
day that I arranged to talk to General Scott about
these fruits, I saw on the news that the old man had
died in his sleep. Never will forget the scene at the
White House. Why, those sons of bitches were all
celebrating, and saying rotten things about Dean Clift,
the new President, and how he was pussy-whipped
by his wife Elizabeth, and how he would spend all
of his time changing clothes while they ran the country, and how Dean Clift was so dumb that he thought
that the Civil War was fought in Canada and that
the South had won. I mean, granted, the guy wasn't
the smartest person in the world, but he was our
president and I thought we should rally around the
guy no matter what.

I admired Elizabeth. She saw to it that her husband
wasn't humiliated all that much. She'd write letters
to the *Washington Sun* when some of these smartass liberal columnists would ridicule the poor bastard.
But between you and me, they were right. He spent
all of his time in the family quarters watching television and movies. She and Reverend Jones got into
it about this soothsayer that Elizabeth was always
consulting. He wanted to drive her out of Washington. You know the rest. She died while lighting the
White House christmas tree. I'm convinced that Jones

had something to do with it. They liquidated the secretary of defense, I know that for a fact.

Things really began to get strange then. Something came over Clift after Elizabeth died. You know how he shocked the nation when he went on television and without a single gaffe, without stumbling all over his mouth, told us about the Terrible Twos plan, the plan to hit Nigeria with H-bombs and wipe out the surplus population in the U.S. as well. Shocked the hell out of me to see the guy making that speech without his usual cue cards, and relying on his smile, and that Redford mug that was responsible for his being in politics in the first place. I was wondering how the guy knew. When he said he got the news from Santa Claus, Jones and Krantz were able to put him away. After Clift left, there were rumors of auras being seen all over the White House. There was even talk that Jones was consulting a departed S.S. officer about the affairs of state and hired some kind of robot to deal with his enemies. There were Nazis in the Bush campaign back there in 1988, but none of them was an actual S.S. officer, a dead S.S. officer at that. I didn't see anything because it was about that time that Jones and I began to quarrel. They stopped inviting me to meetings. I thought it was bad enough that he usurped the powers of Dean Clift, but he was using Jesse Hatch, that pathetic clown who succeeded Clift.

But what really worries me is Kingsley Scab, Hatch's vice president. Next to him, Reverend Jones may someday seem like a lovable crank. This guy has

really got some shady connections. The guys don't
take him seriously. They call him Gucci Two Shoes
behind his back, and make fun of his womanish
manners, which didn't surprise me because, regardless of their gay-bashing, the conservative movement
is loaded with queers. But I think this guy has some
crazy plans for the country, and if he ever gained
power, God help us. He never said a thing when
Jones and the rest attended these meetings, clearly
out of their minds. He just sat there with his patrician
sneer, in those white slacks and black blazer, toying
with his Phi Beta Kappa key. A Yalie. But I could
tell that he had nothing but contempt for these guys.
Sure, he tried to come on like a regular fellow, quoting the ball scores and all that and wearing good-
old-boy caps, and bragging about his recipe for Texas
Red, and bowling with the secret service, but I saw
through it. One of my friends in the C.I.A. told me
that Scab belongs to some secret organization called
the Sons of New England or some such thing. They
meet in secret and read poetry by some guy named
Robert Frost. I'm an Edgar Guest man myself.

Why didn't I come to the country with what I
knew? Call a press conference? Why did I wait so
long? Well, you remember all of those books that
came out about Dutch, the traitor who negotiated
with the reds back there in the late 80s? They clearly
damaged the office of the Presidency, and I thought,
even if these guys around Scott were fools, they were
our fools. But now I've just about had it. Things have
become so weird in the White House that I plan to
call a press conference tomorrow and spill all I know

about the Terrible Twos. Yeah, you guessed it. Clift
was right. But I didn't say anything because I wanted
to stay on and see how far these guys would go. Clift
dug a hole for himself when he said that Nicholas
told him. I guess he had to say that in order to protect
his deep throat, but I tell ya, when he made that
speech that night, I started to join him. I didn't do
it because I just didn't think that the country could
take another scandal after Nixon, Reagan and Bush,
then Clift's removal from office. But now is the time
to break the scandal.

Tonight I'm going to be roasted at the press club.
Bob Krantz is picking me and the missus up. I've
grown fond of the kid, much to Reverend Jones'
annoyance. Reverend Jones thinks he owns Bob since
he saved his life. I'm trying to tell him that Reverend
Jones doesn't own him. And that he should break
from Jones. If they knew I was writing this letter
they'd—oh damn, somebody's at the door. I had to
put some double locks on. The missus said that she
saw some guys prowling around the neighborhood.
People have been calling recently, but when I pick
up the phone they hang up.

After serving thirty days, Elder Marse had been released
from Club Fed for good behavior, and had announced his
plan to inaugurate Xmas Forever, a plan that would draw
shoppers to the department stores all year around . . . Rock
and roll star Boy Junior had announced to the world his find
of a winged reptile fossil proving that birds descended from
the dinosaurs. The D'Roaches, a derisive term given the
Amerikander Party led by a forty-year-old skinhead named

Termite Control, was gaining in the polls, but all of the pundits agreed that this party, which was on the ballot in twelve states, didn't have a chance. The American people weren't that stupid. Jesse Hatch and Reverend Jones called for national unity and promised that the kidnapers of Dean Clift would be brought to justice . . . Tonight, Xmas Night, Reverend Jones would lead the nation in prayer for the recovery from the Terribles which have plagued the nation since Dallas, November 22, 1963.

Oakland, California
November 7, 1988

DALKEY ARCHIVE PAPERBACKS

Visit our website: www.dalkeyarchive.com

DALKEY ARCHIVE PAPERBACKS

Visit our website: www.dalkeyarchive.com

Dalkey Archive Press
ISU Campus Box 4241, Normal, IL 61790–4241
fax (309) 438–7422